UNLOCKING THE POWER OF GRACE

HOW RELIGION USES
THE BIBLE AGAINST US

DEREK MITCHELL

UNLOCKING THE POWER OF GRACE
HOW RELIGION USES THE BIBLE AGAINST US

Cover design by Yvonne Parks at www.pearcreative.ca

Printed in the United States of America

ENDORSEMENTS

"Derek is a young, anointed vessel. He is able to process spiritual concepts, break them down, and put feet on them for people. Derek has a big trumpet to blow for the body of Christ, one that will cultivate a passion for the gospel of grace and captivate. He has taken things we've all heard before and turned them into a revelation. Derek writes with a spirit that convinces you of God's goodness and of the infinite possibilities we have in Christ."

— Sean Smith, Sean Smith Ministries/Pointblank International,
Author of *I Am Your Sign*

"For something that has been the foundation of my faith for over thirty years, it's amazing how much I learned about grace in this book. Derek skillfully takes Bible passages that we have found a way to complicate, and humbly brings us back to the heart of the text. Whether you're a seasoned follower of Jesus looking to better understand God's greatest gift or someone newly exploring what it means to be forgiven and set free by God, I think you will find your own story in these pages."

— Chris Coli, Pastor

"The Good News of the Gospel is so extraordinarily good that if you try to figure it all out with your mind instead of receiving it in your spirit, it will seem too good to be true. Derek does a masterful job of revealing the hidden treasures of God's grace and love that can be found within even the most 'troubling' passages in the Bible. The insights he shares will help you break through the chains of fear and performance to discover the tender heart your heavenly Father has towards you. Allow your spirit to drink it in.

"Derek's ongoing discovery of the extreme goodness of God is one that we are all invited to enjoy. I encourage you to go on a journey of exploration with the Holy Spirit leading you as you read through *Unlocking the Power of*

Grace. Allow yourself to be drawn into the wonder of belonging to the God who has set His full affections upon you as his son or daughter.

"Thank you, Derek, for having the courage to express your heart so that others can be set free to explore the endless sea of the love of Jesus."

— Brent R. Lokker, Pastor and Author of *Always Loved:*
You Are God's Treasure, Not His Project

"I am always surprised at how little Christians understand about *grace*, especially since it is the core of the gospel message. Too often the liberating power of grace is lost in the wearisome effort of trying harder to do better. Christianity is not about human performance but about the power of Christ at work in our lives. I am thankful for Derek's efforts toward helping us see this truth."

— John Merritt, Pastor

"This is a powerful and thought-provoking book that some might find a bit controversial. It will definitely get you thinking and talking about the Old Covenant vs. the New. Derek skillfully walks us through the Bible and exposes what grace really is, reminding us that it's all there is. He draws from his own personal experience as he shows us how to look at many difficult Scriptures through the "lenses" of grace, speaking to the hunger we all have for security and for understanding. I must say, after reading it, I felt a great sense of God's comforting presence surrounding me. If you have **ever** been unsure of your salvation for **any** reason, this book is for you!"

— Sondra Perry,
Entrepreneur, Author

"It has been my pleasure to watch Derek and his family walk out their relationship with God for many years. I have witnessed first hand how he navigated the rough waters of biblical legalism to ultimately land on the beautiful shores of God's amazing grace. I highly recommend this book to anyone who has ever wondered if God's grace is truly sufficient for them. I believe the book you hold in your hands will change your life if you read it with an expectation of transformation."

— Drew Berlfein,
Itinerant Minister

"Derek does a great job of unpacking God's new covenant message of grace. He exposes the legalism that still plagues modern Christianity while dispelling the myth that living under total grace is a license to sin. I wholeheartedly recommend this book to anyone who wants solid, biblical evidence that when Jesus saves us He does so once and for all."

— David Haubert, Business Executive,
Political Public Servant

DEDICATION

This book is dedicated to all who have ever been hurt, misled, or disillusioned by people using the Bible to misrepresent God's heart of unfailing love and unlimited mercy.

ACKNOWLEDGMENTS

To my wife, Cynthia: Thank you for your intense love, encouragement, and faithfulness. Without your belief in me (and an occasional kick in the rear), this book would have stayed just an idea that seemed too lofty for me.

To Brent Lokker and Blazing Fire Church: Thank you for teaching me what grace really means and for honoring the different journeys we all get to take.

To my review team: Your feedback was invaluable for fine-tuning the message. Thank you so much for investing your time and your hearts!

TABLE OF CONTENTS

INTRODUCTION

Insecure. Powerless. Distant. These are some words that describe what many people feel about their relationship with God. There are countless numbers of us who have been misled into thinking that if we fall short in our faith in some way, then we might not make it to heaven. At times, we can be unsure about our salvation altogether. We can wonder if we have measured up to the minimum acceptable level of faith or if we have drifted too far away in our hearts to still be saved.

Why don't we feel close to God? Where is the power we read about in the Bible? Are we walking close enough to God to keep our salvation? What does God think or feel about me?

This is a book for all of us who are looking to walk more intimately with God and to experience more of His power and presence. It is for those of us who want to know for sure that we are loved and accepted just the way we are; who want to stand tall and be confident in who God made us to be.

Many of us have been hurt and disillusioned by religion, but we still yearn to know the Creator of the universe on a personal level. We have felt the frustration and discouragement of constantly striving to meet certain "biblical" expectations, and yet we long to know more about the love, grace, freedom, and happiness we sense is available to us. Some of us have simply given up on Christianity: disgusted by hypocrisy, condemned by leaders, and burned out by the endless treadmill of trying to measure up.

Bono (lead singer of the band U2) once said, "Religion is what happens when the Spirit has left the building."[1] Too much of Christianity has come under the spirit of religion by not allowing the Spirit of God the freedom to lead. We can easily know the Holy Spirit is present when there is

> **Galatians 5:22-23** – ...love, joy, peace, patience, kindness, goodness, faithfulness, gentleness, and self-control.

Not only are these the fruits of the Holy Spirit, they are also words that describe God's character, and they should be words that describe the people who know Him as well.

The spirit of religion is the opposite of these. It promotes judgment, oppression, condemnation, accusation, self-righteousness, hatred, and fear. It is this type of religion that is destructive and kills our souls. It deceives us into thinking we are defending God's honor—taking a stand for what we think is right and opposing what we think is wrong—when in reality we are being led away from His heart, which is full of grace.

It's time to break free from the spirit of religion and put an end to these destructive ways. Religion is evil and shackles us to the fear of not being good enough. (When we talk about *religion* in this book, we are referring to that which is influenced by the spirit of religion, which is from the devil, and not about the pure, godly religion spoken of in James 1.) Instead, let's align ourselves with the Spirit of Truth. He is good and frees us from this fear with unconditional love.

We know the truth when we hear it because it makes us come alive in our hearts. Truth breathes joy into us. It is healing and liberating. Truth is power.

John 14:6 – (Jesus speaking) *"I am the truth."*

Jesus is the truth that reveals God's heart. He was continually mobbed by thousands of people because life, joy, healing, freedom, and power flowed out from Him, Simply put, **Jesus was love wrapped in flesh.**

Our goal is to get to know **this** Jesus better, to learn more about who He really is and what He really did for us. To accomplish this we will look at the true, biblical meaning of grace and see if there are any limits to it. We will dissect Bible passages that seem to contradict this amazing grace and determine if they should be translated or interpreted differently. We will also see if the enemy has distorted our perception of the Bible to promote religion and all of its trappings. Hopefully, before the end of our time together, we will get to the heart of God and see what's really inside.

But doing all of this might require us to look at the Bible in a different light than we are used to. It might mean that we open ourselves up to other perspectives—ones that might go against our current beliefs.

> God will never contradict His Word, but He doesn't mind contradicting my understanding of it. In fact, He seems to take pleasure in it.[2] Bill Johnson

If God will never contradict His Word, why do there seem to be Scriptures that contradict each other?

Is it possible to reconcile Bible verses that seem to contradict the meaning of grace with those that say grace is unlimited and everlasting? Verses like

> **Matthew 13:20-21** – *The one who received the seed that fell on rocky places is the man who hears the word and at once receives it with joy. But since he has no root, he lasts only a short time. When trouble or persecution comes because of the word, he quickly **falls away.***

Galatians 5:19-21 – *The acts of the sinful nature are obvious: sexual immorality, impurity and debauchery; idolatry and witchcraft; hatred, discord, jealousy, fits of rage, selfish ambition, dissensions, factions and envy; drunkenness, orgies, and the like.* ***I warn you, as I did before, that those who live like this will not inherit the kingdom of God.***

1 Corinthians 5:19-21 – *By this gospel you are saved,* ***if you hold firmly to the word I preached to you. Otherwise, you have believed in vain.***

(all emphasis mine)

As compared with passages like

Romans 8:38-39 – *For I am convinced that neither death nor life, neither angels nor demons, neither the present nor the future, nor any powers, neither height nor depth, nor* ***anything else in all creation, will be able to separate us from the love of God that is in Christ*** *Jesus our Lord.*

Hebrews 8:12 – *Their sins and lawless acts* ***I will remember no more.***

Hebrews 10:10 – *...**we have been made holy** through the sacrifice of the body of Jesus Christ **once for all.***

(all emphasis mine)

These conflicting messages raise many questions. How can we be made holy by the blood of Jesus but then be defiled again by sin? That sounds like sin is more powerful than Jesus' blood. Do we go back and forth between being saved and lost depending on what sins we commit? Or is it possible for us to be secure and confident in our salvation no matter what? The Scriptures seem to indicate both.

The passages in the New Testament that appear to say we can lose our salvation do not fit with the definition of grace, which is undeserved and unmerited favor. They are not consistent with what the Bible says Jesus accomplished on the cross. Something is being mistranslated, misinterpreted, or misunderstood. How can grace be grace if we can lose it? It can't be both. If we can lose it, then we are not saved by grace but rather by how we live (i.e. how well we obey, what we do, whether our lives measure up to a certain standard, etc.). This is what Paul called living under the law, not grace.

Okay, but why is this so important? It's important because if we can lose our salvation, then we will never experience the true peace, freedom, intimacy, joy, power, and authority that grace really offers and that the Bible says is ours. An accurate understanding of grace has everything to do with how we relate to God, how close we feel to Him, and how much we are able to enjoy Him. It's the basis of how we live our entire lives. Additionally, it determines how big of an impact we can have on the world.

How Did We Get Here?

Not long after the first century came to an end, the church began to get increasingly more institutionalized. Leadership put a greater focus on management and less of a focus on intimacy with God and spiritual gifts. The religious spirit began a long evolutionary process to rid the church of its spiritual power by shifting back to the rule-keeping paradigm of the Old Covenant.

In the early 4th century, with the conversion of Constantine, the church and the government were joined together. Many people joined the church for political and financial gain instead of a desire to satisfy their spiritual hunger for salvation and purpose. Since then, much of our theological heritage has been influenced by centuries of corruption and political maneuvering.

The following excerpt is from an article on the history of the English Bible:

> By 500 AD, the Bible had been translated into over 500 languages. Just one century later, by 600 AD, it had been restricted to only one language: the Latin Vulgate! The only organized and recognized

church at that time in history was the Catholic Church of Rome, and they refused to allow the scripture to be available in any language other than Latin. Those in possession of non-Latin scriptures would be executed! This was because only the priests were educated to understand Latin, and this gave the church ultimate power...a power to rule without question...a power to deceive...a power to extort money from the masses. Nobody could question their "Biblical" teachings, because few people other than priests could read Latin. The church capitalized on this forced-ignorance through the 1,000 year period from 400 AD to 1,400 AD known as the "Dark and Middle Ages."

Pope Leo the Tenth established a practice called the "selling of indulgences" as a way to extort money from the people. He offered forgiveness of sins for a fairly small amount of money. For a little bit more money, you would be allowed to indulge in a continuous lifestyle of sin, such as keeping a mistress. Also, through the invention of "Purgatory," you could purchase the salvation of your loved-one's souls. The church taught the ignorant masses, "As soon as the coin in the coffer rings, the troubled soul from Purgatory springs!" Pope Leo the Tenth showed his true feelings when he said, "The fable of Christ has been quite profitable to us!"[3]

(The intent here is not to discredit the Catholic Church. It is just the truth of history. Many great men and women of God were and are part of the Catholic Church.)

In his book, *The New Mystics,* John Crowder says, "We need to have the eyes of our heart enlightened by the Holy Spirit. It is better to still have questions than to have wrong answers. How many demonic doctrines have crept into the church because of theologians who interpreted the Bible out of human wisdom, with a predetermined theological agenda?"[4]

It is a shame that some of the doctrines formed in the Dark Ages still influence our theology today. These roots of religion have spread deep and wide over that thousand year period and can be very difficult for the church of our day to break free of.

Hide and Seek

Fortunately, ever-increasing revelations of God's heart of love and grace continue to be released as we complete these last days. He is returning the *good* to the good news. As a result, we are in the midst of a grace revolution. It's not that people are throwing out sound theology, but rather that the Holy Spirit is revealing deeper truths of the Scriptures, things kept hidden until the right time.

> **Proverbs 25:2** – *It is the glory of God to conceal a matter; to search out a matter is the glory of kings.*

Some of us are being prompted by the Spirit to search out the depths of His grace.

> **1 Corinthians 2:10** – *The Spirit searches [examines] all things, even the deep [hidden] things of God.* (brackets mine)

The time is at hand for His church to understand the finished work of the cross, so that we can walk in complete confidence of our salvation. This will embolden us to live and love with power and authority, just like Jesus, the apostles, and the great men and women of faith throughout history.

Let's ask our heavenly Father for a fresh revelation of what the cross really accomplished and allow the Holy Spirit to teach us like Jesus said He would.

> **John 14:26** – *"But the Counselor, the Holy Spirit, whom the Father will send in my name, will teach you all things."*

Join me in praying something like, "OK, Papa, if there is something in the Bible that You want me to think differently about, then please reveal it to me. I am choosing to trust You instead of leaning on my own understanding (Proverbs 3:5). I ask You to make things clear to me at the right time."

We are set to embark on an exciting journey through the Scriptures and to unlock the transforming power of grace.

Parts to the Whole

In Part I, we will look at the overall context of the Scriptures, as well as the context of different sections of the Bible, in order to lay the foundation for the paradigm of the New Covenant.

In Part II, we are going to examine grace in greater detail, looking at different facets of what the Bible says it is and what it includes.

In Part III, we will review several Scriptures that seem to contradict grace, take them apart, examine some of the Greek, and see how they might be translated (or at least viewed) differently, so that they are consistent with what Jesus accomplished for us.

It is not completely necessary to read Parts I and II before reading Part III. Feel free to jump ahead. The chapters in Part III can stand on their own and were the original inspiration for the whole book.

Blessing

I bless you on your journey to know His heart of grace in deeper and deeper ways, and I sincerely hope this book will be a great help to that end.

PART I

CONTEXT IS EVERYTHING

Chapter 1:
Context of the Old Covenant

Context enables us to make sense of things. It includes the facts or circumstances surrounding whatever information we are trying to process. If we have no context for information, then our minds will search for something to relate it to so that we can attempt to understand it. If we don't come up with anything, we tend to ignore it because there is nothing in our mind for it to attach itself to; we just don't know what to do with it.

But if we relate this new information to the wrong thing, then it could lead us off in a totally different direction than what was intended. Context is everything. And, where the Bible is concerned, if we take the text out of context, we are left with a con—something the enemy can use to deceive us.

We see an example of this right from the start with how the serpent deceived Eve.

> **Genesis 3:1** – *He [the serpent] said to the woman, "Did God really say, 'You must not eat from any tree in the garden'?"* (brackets mine)

From the very beginning, the devil has taken God's words out of context and twisted them into lies. He veers off track just enough to make it still sound right, but he really says something God never meant nor implied. Many great human tragedies and atrocities throughout history were sparked by people being deceived and taking Bible verses out of context. They went spinning off recklessly toward destruction and took many innocent lives with them.

The Word of God is extremely powerful. It created everything in the entire universe. Power used incorrectly is dangerous and the enemy knows this. That is why we must make sure we understand the context of His Word. Context gives us boundaries to channel this power for its intended purposes. The more we understand the context, the more clear the picture becomes of what was trying to be communicated and why.

The context of the Old Covenant at the time Jesus was born was that of being under the law, which meant people needed to obey all of the commandments perfectly or be condemned. This model began centuries earlier with Moses when the Israelites rejected God's offer to have a relationship with Him.

God offered his people the chance to have a relationship with Him similar similar to the one He had with Moses—one of friendship and interaction. But the only paradigm the Israelites had of God was from the stories that were handed down through the ages, the amazing signs that He did through Moses, and the dark cloud that sat on top of Mt. Sinai with thunder and lightning coming out of it. They didn't really know His heart, and so, in fear, they decided to let God keep telling Moses what they should do, and they promised they would do it.

> **Exodus 20:18-19** – *When the people saw the thunder and lightning and heard the trumpet and saw the mountain in smoke, they trembled with fear. They stayed at a distance and said to Moses, "Speak to us yourself and we will listen. But do not have God speak to us or we will die."*

When they rejected intimacy with Him, they reduced their relationship to law keeping.

The law spelled out what Israel had to do in order to be righteous before God—to be acceptable in the presence of His perfection. Since they chose not to trust God's goodness when He offered them a relationship, they now had to trust in their own efforts by attempting to measure up to God's standard. Instead of a friendship with God, they entered into a performance-based contract where there was constant striving for acceptance and security. But in such an arrangement, even love becomes measured.

> **Mark 12:30** – (Jesus speaking) *"Love the Lord your God with all your heart and with all your soul and with all your mind and with all your strength."*

Jesus is quoting the most important commandment of the Old Covenant from Deuteronomy 6:5. If we really consider what He's saying, we will realize this is impossible. While on one hand this command expresses God's desire to have a close intimate relationship with us, on the other hand, it's worded in a way that no one can achieve it. We will all fall short. There will always be something else we could have done to love God more. This "always falling short" is the curse of the law; it's the treadmill of always needing to live up to a standard but never being able to.

> **Galatians 3:10** – *All who rely on observing the law are under a curse, for it is written: "Cursed is everyone who does not continue to do everything written in the Book of the Law."*

> **James 2:10** – *For whoever keeps the whole law and yet stumbles at just one point is guilty of breaking all of it.*

These verses imply that unless they were able to keep the entire law perfectly, all the time, they were just as guilty as someone who broke every law. **Everyone who tried to meet the standard of the law was under a curse because they were burdened with the unbearable load of always trying to live up to an unattainable expectation.**

God was not being mean by giving the Israelites the law. He was responding to their pride of thinking they could do everything He said. Obviously they didn't realize the implications of their decision. But over time, He continued to reveal more and more of His desire to be a Father and not a Master.

Hints of Grace

Even though the law was very stiff and unyielding, God still showed a lot of grace because of His prior covenant with Abraham. If not for this grace, the entire nation of Israel would have been wiped out.

For example, when Moses came down the mountain with the Ten Commandments and saw that the people were worshipping an idol, he smashed the tablets before entering the camp. If the law had entered the camp while their blatant idolatry was under way, they might have all been killed. Instead, only 3000 died for their iniquity. God showed His heart of grace even in the midst of giving the law. By smashing the tablets Moses also foreshadowed both the end of the law and the introduction of grace that would come with the New Covenant.

God foreshadowed New Covenant grace again with the initiation of the annual sacrifice of Atonement. Along with the law, God established a system of sacrifices whereby mercy would be extended to those who did not intentionally break the law. In God's justice system, blood had to be spilled in order for sin not to be held against the sinner. Families would typically sacrifice a perfect lamb through a ceremony in which their sinfulness, guilt, and shame were transferred to the lamb, and the innocence and perfection of the lamb was, in turn, attributed to the family. This would happen once a year, every year, on the Day of Atonement. (To *atone* for something means to make up for a mistake and be reconciled to the offended party.)

The family offering the sacrifice did not have to do anything other than agree to their sinfulness and offer a perfect sacrifice. The priest would not inspect the family in order to see if they were really sorry and committed to change their ways. He would only inspect the lamb. As long as the lamb was worthy, the sacrifice was accepted and the family's sin was atoned for.

Obviously, this is a picture of what Jesus did for us, but many of us are not satisfied with His sacrifice alone. We want to examine ourselves, and each other as well, to see if we qualify for Jesus' sacrifice to apply to our sin. This is offensive to the perfection of the sacrifice. It says we think the sacrifice is lacking in power to completely cover us just as we are, that it is insufficient in some way, and that we need to contribute something as well. Whenever we look to ourselves to add something to the sacrifice of Jesus so that we will be accepted by the Father, we imply that what Jesus did was not good enough. The context of a sacrifice is that it satisfies everything necessary for the guilty party to be reconciled to the offended party. Nothing more is needed.

However, if someone intentionally broke the law in the Old Covenant, their punishment was death. As ironic as it may sound, this is also a foreshadowing of the New Covenant of grace.

> **1 Corinthians 5:14** – *[Jesus] died for all, and therefore all died.* (bracket mine)

> **Galatians 2:20** – *[we] have been crucified with Christ* (bracket mine)

> **Romans 6:3** – *all of us who were baptized into Christ Jesus were baptized into his death.*

Jesus' death was our death. We died with Him. As a result, His sacrifice covers both our unintentional and intentional sins.

Grace Out of Context

Another example of God's grace in the Old Covenant is David. The amazing thing about David was that he had what appears to be a New Covenant relationship of grace with God in an Old Covenant context. More than once, David intentionally broke laws and yet did not receive the punishment he deserved. There were definitely consequences to his sins, but, under the law, his punishment for committing adultery with Bathsheba and then arranging for her husband to be killed should have been death.

David was a forerunner, a prophetic glimpse of who we could be and what we could have in the New Covenant. He showed that we would be kings and queens in the kingdom of God. He also showed that we would have an intimate relationship with our heavenly Daddy based on grace, not law.

One consequence for David's sin was the death of the child that was conceived in the adulterous affair with Bathsheba. Another consequence was that violence would always be a part of his life. But because David's relationship with God was founded on grace, God turned right around and anointed their next child as heir to the throne even though he was not the next in line to receive the crown. King Solomon went on to become the wisest, richest king ever, and his kingdom knew nothing but peace throughout his reign. It was the pinnacle of Israel's kingdom in the Old Testament.

This is a beautiful picture of grace: unmerited and undeserved favor. Grace takes our mistakes and makes things turn out better than they ever would have before we made the mistake in the first place. It turns our deserts into springs, our rocky roads into smooth highways. With grace

> **Romans 8:28** – ...*we know that in all things God works for the good of those who love him.*

Why did God call David a man after His own heart? Because David experienced and understood that His heart was full of grace. David sought to really know Him, to encounter Him, to find out what He was really like. David came to know God's heart to be kind, compassionate, slow to anger, abounding in love, etc. and so God showered him with favor.

One amazing fruit of their grace-based relationship was that David worshiped God with freedom and joy. He sang, he danced, he celebrated God's faithfulness and mercy, and he prophetically showed us the kind of worshipers the Father seeks.

John 4:23 – *(Jesus speaking) "a time is coming and has now come when the true worshipers will worship the Father in spirit and truth, for **they are the kind of worshipers the Father seeks**."* (emphasis and brackets mine)

Worshiping in spirit and truth is all about exalting God's goodness, praising His faithfulness, and glorifying His everlasting love because worship is about rejoicing in what He has done for us. The word *truth* here means not hiding anything. It is not speaking of doctrine, but rather of us worshiping God as we really are, coming to Him as our flawed selves and celebrating His acceptance of us.

David was simply reflecting back **to** God the kind of love he felt **from** God.

Zephaniah 3:17 – *...He will take great delight in you, he will quiet you with his love, he will rejoice over you with singing.*

The word translated *rejoice* here implies that God is leaping and dancing while He is also singing over us. Isn't that amazing? The Father takes such great delight in us, just as we are, that He sings a love song to us and, at the same time, is so overjoyed that He can't help but dance over us, too. This is the heart of our heavenly Daddy! The more we grasp how joyful and giddy God is for us in His grace, the more we will celebrate with singing and dancing in worship toward Him.

This verse, like so many of David's psalms, speaks of New Covenant realities centuries before they came into being.

Psalm 32:1-2 – *Blessed is he whose transgressions are forgiven, whose sins are covered. Blessed is the man whose sin the Lord does not count against him*

The greatest blessing available to us is to be forgiven—to have the Lord not count our sins against us.

David had a deep conviction that God's heart was full of grace, and he wanted everyone to experience it for themselves. He was completely confident of God's everlasting faithfulness to him no matter where he went or what he did.

> **Psalm 139:7** – *Where can I go from your Spirit? Where can I flee from your presence?*

He knew that God would always be with him no matter what. In the New Covenant, His Spirit and His Presence are available for all of us to experience and enjoy everyday. God will never leave us or forsake us. Even if we try to flee or run away, He will remain faithful.

> **Psalm 23:6** – *Surely goodness and love [mercy] will follow me all the days of my life, and I will dwell in the house of the Lord forever.* (bracket mine)

When this passage speaks of God's goodness and mercy following us, it carries the implication that they will chase us or hunt us down. We simply can't escape because He is that faithful, that persistent, that determined to have us know Him.

David even knew that his life with God was predestined, established in eternity, unable to be altered by circumstances in the realm of time.

> **Psalm 139:7** – *All the days ordained for me were written in your book before one of them came to be.*

If someone under an inferior covenant could know God in such a way, how much more should we walk in the glory of His grace?

Ministry of Death

So now we have this mixture of law and grace in the Old Covenant, with the law representing man's striving to measure up, and grace representing God's everlasting mercy. These are also pictures of life by the flesh (or sinful nature) and life by the Spirit. They are at odds with each other. Law vs. grace; flesh vs. Spirit; death vs. life; sin vs. righteousness. When there is a mixture of law and grace, there is conflict.

> **Galatians 5:17-18** – *For the sinful nature desires what is contrary to the Spirit, and the Spirit what is contrary to the sinful nature. They are in conflict with each other, so that you do not do what you want. But if you are led by the Spirit, you are not under law.*

And look at how He went on to further describe this mixture.

> **2 Corinthians 3:6-7** – *...the letter [the law] kills, but the Spirit gives life. Now if the ministry that brought death, which was engraved in letters on stone...* (brackets mine)

It is almost shocking how God calls the Old Covenant (i.e. the mixture of law and grace) the ministry of death! He says that the law kills us and it's the Spirit that gives us life. When there is a standard that we must try to live up to, along with the threat of punishment if we don't, even if grace is available, we will eventually fall under its weight and crumble under its pressure. It brings death to our souls and spirits. We can't be who He made us to be in that kind of environment. We simply don't thrive.

Because the mixture of law and grace brings spiritual death, God ended the Old Covenant and started the New. He introduced the New Covenant so that we wouldn't have to strive anymore. His acceptance of us is completely based on His grace. In the Ten Commandments God said, "You shall not... you shall not...you shall not." But in the New Covenant He says, "I will...I will...I will" **(Exodus 20:3-17 vs. Jeremiah 31:33-34)**. Thus, He declared the Old Covenant obsolete.

> **Hebrews 8:7, 13** – *For if there had been nothing wrong with that first covenant, no place would have been sought for another...By calling this covenant "new," he has made the first one obsolete...*

The Old Covenant is dead. In the New Covenant, He removes the law from us because it was fulfilled by Jesus on our behalf. Since it has been fulfilled, it is no longer needed.

The context of the Old Covenant was being under the law with some foreshadowing of grace sprinkled in. The law incorporates the concept that we must live up to a certain expectation in order to qualify for righteousness before God. Even though God has called this covenant obsolete, many Christians today still believe we must meet a standard of righteousness in order to be a candidate for salvation or in order to keep our salvation intact. This is Old Covenant, law-based theology and has no place in the New Covenant of grace.

In the next chapter, we reveal how the Gospels are not what many of us thought.

CHAPTER 2:
CONTEXT OF THE GOSPELS

Galatians 4:4 – *But when the time had fully come, God sent his Son, born of a woman, born under law...*

Jesus was born under the Old Covenant of law. The New Covenant did not start until He died, so Jesus lived and ministered in an Old Covenant context. He had to keep the law perfectly (i.e. never sin or fall short) His entire life in order to fulfill it on our behalf. He also had to obey the law completely so that He would qualify as a perfect offering to remove the stain of our sin from us.

A point of confusion for many believers is thinking that the Gospels are part of the New Covenant when they are not. Even though they are included in the New Testament part of the Bible, the life and ministry of Jesus took place in the Old Covenant context of being under the law. This point cannot be stressed enough.

Think of the Gospels as the transition period from Old to New Covenants. Before Jesus went to the cross, He was closing out the Old Covenant and introducing the New. It was a time of transition. I like how Doug Addison (prophetic evangelist) defines a period of transition, "It's when the old isn't working anymore, but the new hasn't started yet,"[5] which describes Jesus' life perfectly.

Because Jesus was living under the law, not everything He said applies to us who now live under the grace of the New Covenant. Some of what He said was directed at Old Covenant issues and some of it was at New. He spoke on both sides of the fence because He was wrapping up the Old and starting up the New. **However, if we look at the things Jesus said in the right context and rely on the Holy Spirit, we can certainly benefit from everything He said.**

In order for the Old Covenant to end and the New Covenant to start, Jesus had to die. It takes a death to end a biblical covenant and a blood sacrifice to begin one. Jesus did both at once.

One proof of this radical change from Old to New, from law to grace, was that when Jesus died, the earth shook; the veil of the temple that separated us from His presence was literally torn in two; and many holy men and women rose from the dead, came out of their tombs, and appeared to people. God couldn't have made a more emphatic statement to announce this new eternal covenant!

The Law Side of the Fence

Many of us on the New Covenant side of the cross know that we can never satisfy the law. Man simply cannot measure up to it. But on the Old Covenant side of the cross, they didn't know this, so they worked very hard at following all the laws in an attempt to be righteous. Jesus speaks to this point in the story of the Rich Young Man.

> **Mark 10:17-22** – *As Jesus started on his way, a man ran up to him and fell on his knees before him. "Good teacher," he asked, "what must I do to inherit eternal life?"*

"Why do you call me good?" Jesus answered. "No one is good—except God alone. You know the commandments: 'Do not murder, do not commit adultery, do not steal, do not give false testimony, do not defraud, honor your father and mother.'"

"Teacher," he declared, "all these I have kept since I was a boy."

Jesus looked at him and loved him. "One thing you lack," he said. "Go, sell everything you have and give to the poor, and you will have treasure in heaven. Then come, follow me."

At this the man's face fell. He went away sad, because he had great wealth.

When this man asked Jesus what he must do to inherit eternal life, Jesus didn't say, "Believe that I am the Son of God," which would have been a New Covenant answer. He basically said, "Obey the commandments," which is an Old Covenant response. The rich young man was excited because he thought he had kept them all since his youth. But then Jesus tells him that he's still lacking one thing; he needs to sell everything he has, give it to the poor, and follow Him.

Is this the gospel? Do we need to obey the commandments for salvation? Do we need to sell everything and give it to the poor in order to become Christians? Obviously not. One of the things Jesus was doing was revealing the nature of the law. When we think we've measured up to it, the law always says, "Oh, you still lack one thing..." because we can never be righteous on our own. The standard is just too high.

One of the purposes of the law was for us to see our sinfulness and that we need a Savior to measure up for us.

Romans 3:20 – *...through the law we become conscious of sin.*

When we are always striving to meet a standard, we constantly look at where we are falling short. That's how the law makes us conscious of sin. Our mistakes are always on our minds, nagging us that we are not good enough and yet pointing us to our need for Jesus.

The rich young man hadn't seen his need for a Savior yet and was still trying to do it on his own. He was still trying to fulfill the law, so when he asked a law-based question, Jesus gave him a law-based answer.

Now, even though Jesus is addressing an Old Covenant law issue, we can still learn things from this story, just like we can from stories in the Old Testament.

Another time Jesus challenged Old Covenant thinking was in the famous Sermon on the Mount starting in Matthew 5:17 and continuing on until the end of Chapter 7. We will just look at a couple of verses as an example.

> **Matthew 5:21-22** – *"You have heard that it was said to the people long ago, 'Do not murder, and anyone who murders will be subject to judgment.' But I tell you that anyone who is angry with his brother will be subject to judgment. Again, anyone who says to his brother, 'Raca,' is answerable to the Sanhedrin. But anyone who says, 'You fool!' will be in danger of the fire of hell."*

The Word of God is multi-dimensional and multi-faceted, and there are many different ways we can look at and apply these passages. One of the ways we can look at the Sermon on the Mount is from the perspective of those who think they are living up to the standard of the law. The religious rulers and most of the upstanding citizens of the day, like the rich young man we just looked at, believed that they were able to keep the law sufficiently enough to be righteous before God.

In the above passage, Jesus tells them that not murdering someone isn't really the standard, but rather it's not even getting angry with someone. He basically says, "You thought the standard was at this level, but I'm telling you it's way beyond what you could ever live up to. It doesn't just deal with your actions, it deals with what's going on in your heart."

It's no wonder that the religious people were so upset with Him. In essence, what He was saying here stripped them of their whole sense of pride in who they thought they were. They got their identity from obeying the law. They put all of their security in it, and Jesus was pulling the rug right out from under their feet.

One thing Jesus did here was to reveal the true extent of the law, showing that no one could measure up to it.

He was not telling us in the New Covenant what the standard of being a Christian was. Jesus was not saying that the standard for righteousness in the Old Covenant was "do not murder," but now the standard for righteousness in the New Covenant was that you couldn't even get angry with someone or else you were in danger of going to hell. How is that good news? He was not raising the bar to an impossible height for us in the New Covenant. He was trying to point out to those under the law that they were deceived to think that they could ever be righteous by attempting to live up to the standard of the law – especially because they didn't even know what the standard really was (not that they could have done it if they did know).

Again, one of the purposes of the law is to bring us to a place where we realize that we need a Savior; we need someone to obey all the laws for us as well as pay our debt for us.

Jesus goes on to hit several more laws, doing the same thing each time. Not committing the act of adultery isn't the standard. The real measure is not even looking at someone with lust in our hearts. It isn't loving our neighbors, but loving our enemies. Again, these are impossible standards for men and women who have sinful natures.

Then Jesus reveals the bottom line at the end of this part of the sermon.

> **Matthew 5:48 –** *"Be perfect, therefore, as your heavenly Father is perfect."*

This is the real standard that the law sets to be righteous. **We must be perfect in order to be justified with God.**

Obviously perfection is impossible for man but

> **Luke 1:37** – ...*nothing is impossible with God.*

It is only in Jesus that we become perfect.

> **Colossians 1:28** – *We proclaim him...so that we may present everyone perfect in Christ.*

We are perfect because He is perfect. When we accept what He has done for us, His identity before the Father is transferred to us. This is how we go from darkness to light, from lost to saved, from unrighteous to righteous. This is when His perfection becomes our perfection.

For us in the New Covenant, we should certainly do our best to keep the law as Jesus is spelling it out, but not in an attempt to be righteous in God's eyes. We do it because it's right and it honors God. We do it in an attempt to love others like He loves us.

The Grace Side of the Fence

In addition to talking about the law, we also see Jesus extending grace to those who were broken, hurting, lost, and needy. And He did this without requiring anything from them.

> **John 8:2-10** – *At dawn he appeared again in the temple courts, where all the people gathered around him, and he sat down to teach them. The teachers of the law and the Pharisees brought in a woman caught in adultery. They made her stand before the group and said to Jesus, "Teacher, this woman was caught in the act of adultery. In the Law Moses commanded us to stone such women. Now what do you say?" They were using this question as a trap, in order to have a basis for accusing him.*

But Jesus bent down and started to write on the ground with his finger. When they kept on questioning him, he straightened up and said to them, "If any one of you is without sin, let him be the first to throw a stone at her." Again he stooped down and wrote on the ground.

At this, those who heard began to go away one at a time, the older ones first, until only Jesus was left, with the woman still standing there. Jesus straightened up and asked her, "Woman, where are they? Has no one condemned you?"

"No one, sir," she said.

"Then neither do I condemn you," Jesus declared. "Go now and leave your life of sin."

This woman was in a horrible situation. She was being accused of a very embarrassing sin in front of a huge crowd by an angry mob of overbearing, self-righteous hypocrites. And to top it off, she is also facing the death penalty. Luckily for her, they decided to use her situation to try and trap Jesus into saying something contrary to the law in order to discredit Him.

When they charged her with adultery and demanded justice, Jesus bent over and wrote on the ground with His finger. The ground in the temple court was not dirt, it was stone. This was a picture of God writing the Ten Commandments. Jesus remained in this symbolically weak position of stooping down as they continued their accusations. He was showing that when we focus on the law, we will always accuse and condemn each other for our sin.

After Jesus had heard enough, He stood back up to a position of strength and said, *"If any one of you is without sin, let him be the first to throw a stone at her."* These words were full of grace, and yet at the same time they were lovingly confrontational to her accusers. He is saying, "How can you condemn her for her sin when all of you have sin in your own lives as well?" It's a beautiful thing when someone points out our hypocrisy in a way that humbles us but doesn't humiliate us.

As the angry mob reeled from the power of grace and truth, Jesus went back down to the law, perhaps awaiting another round of accusations. But His one sentence was enough to humble their hearts, and they could do nothing but walk away. After they dispersed, Jesus again stood tall and spoke more words of grace. He gave the verdict of "no condemnation" and then told the woman to stop her sinful ways.

In doing so, Jesus reveals that it is God's kindness that leads us toward repentance **(Romans 2:4)**. Unfortunately, in much of the church today, we want people to clean up their lives before we give them a verdict of "no condemnation." (More on repentance in Chapter 4.)

Jesus stood up when He spoke words of grace because grace is always in a stronger position than the law. Grace is always above the law. Like Jesus, grace also makes **us** stand tall and strong because under grace we are accepted just as we are. Like this woman, it is when we receive the verdict of "no condemnation" that we are empowered to overcome sin in our lives. In contrast, as Jesus illustrated, the law bends our backs from the weight of its demands. It makes us weak, unable to overcome because our endless efforts to meet the standard is a load that's too heavy for us to bear.

Another example of Jesus extending grace is in the story of the paralytic who gets lowered through the roof.

> **Mark 2:1-12** – *A few days later, when Jesus again entered Capernaum, the people heard that he had come home. So many gathered that there was no room left, not even outside the door, and he preached the word to them. Some men came, bringing to him a paralytic, carried by four of them. Since they could not get him to Jesus because of the crowd, they made an opening in the roof above Jesus and, after digging through it, lowered the mat the*

paralyzed man was lying on. When Jesus saw their faith, he said to the paralytic, "Son, your sins are forgiven."

Now some teachers of the law were sitting there, thinking to themselves, "Why does this fellow talk like that? He's blaspheming! Who can forgive sins but God alone?"

Immediately Jesus knew in his spirit that this was what they were thinking in their hearts, and he said to them, "Why are you thinking these things? Which is easier: to say to the paralytic, 'Your sins are forgiven,' or to say, 'Get up, take your mat and walk'? But that you may know that the Son of Man has authority on earth to forgive sins..." He said to the paralytic, "I tell you, get up, take your mat and go home." He got up, took his mat and walked out in full view of them all. This amazed everyone and they praised God, saying, "We have never seen anything like this!"

What a great story! The four guys who carried the paralytic are just awesome. It's assumed that all five knew each other, but the four guys could have just walked up to some random guy lying on his mat and picked him up so Jesus could heal him. It doesn't really matter. The great thing is that they had faith that wouldn't be stopped. When they arrived, the house was so crowded that people were spilling out of the doors and they couldn't get the paralytic inside. But they were determined to get this guy in front of Jesus no matter what.

It might have gone something like this:

One of them says, "I know what we can do! Why don't we take him up to the roof, remove the tiles, and lower him down by ropes right in front of Jesus. He will have to heal him then."

The other three shout out, "Let's do it!"

But the paralytic protests, "What?!? Are you guys crazy?! You're going to drop me on my head!"

Another one replies, "So what? Jesus will heal you!"

And the paralytic complies, "Good point. What do I have to lose?"

So Jesus is standing in the middle of the room, teaching everyone about the kingdom of God, and all of a sudden there's a commotion overhead. He stops to see what's going on as the four men make a giant hole in the roof. Some people in the crowd start yelling at them to stop disturbing the Teacher. Jesus waves for the protesters to quiet down and just stands there smiling and watching. The crowd gasps when they see the paralytic dangling in midair by four ropes tied to the corners of his mat. Jesus can't help but chuckle at their child-like faith. When the paralytic finally lands in front of Him, Jesus is so moved by their faith that He doesn't even ask the man if he would like to be healed. He just goes ahead and grants him eternal life.

This story, like all of the stories where Jesus heals people or forgives sin, is as complicated as the gospel of grace gets. **Jesus simply responds with grace to any one of us who turns to Him and trusts Him to help us.** He doesn't require anything from us; He just gives us whatever measure of grace we need, and it's always more than enough.

> **Matthew 8:16** – ...*[Jesus] healed all the sick.*

> **Luke 6:19** – ...*power was coming from him and healing them all.*

No one ever had to do anything to receive grace from Jesus. In the same way, He doesn't require us to clean up our act, confess our sins, or put money in the offering plate. He accepts us just as we are, and because of this we are compelled to draw closer to Him. As we do draw closer, we naturally take on more of His qualities and our desire to sin fades.

Grace is the power that will transform us from victim to victor. The more we embrace and experience it, the more we can become like Jesus.

On the other hand, if we approached Him and He responded with demands that we must first stop doing all of the bad things in our lives and start doing good things before He would forgive us, then we would forever be on a treadmill of trying to measure up to those expectations. We would fight and bicker over what was necessary to qualify. We would judge others if they didn't do what we deemed critical. This is how denominations get formed. Some think that this is repentance, but it's not. It is law. And the heart of Jesus is full of grace to the undeserving.

The context of the Gospels is a transition from Old Covenant to New. We see Jesus teaching on both the law and on grace. If we think everything Jesus said applies to us in the same way it did to His original audience then we are taking the Gospels out of context. We cannot just blindly assume that everything in red letters was said to us because Jesus lived under the law. In order to fulfill the law, He had to uphold it and encourage others to do the same. Even though many things Jesus said do not apply in the New Covenant the same way they did when He said them in the Old, we can benefit from them as we look at them in the right context with the help of the Holy Spirit.

In Chapter 3, we explore how to read and apply the Bible through the lenses of the New Covenant.

CHAPTER 3:
CONTEXT OF THE NEW COVENANT

John 19:30 – *When he had received the drink, Jesus said, "It is finished." With that, he bowed his head and gave up his spirit.*

And thus the New Covenant began.

"It is finished" was more than Jesus announcing His own death. It was a proclamation that had several implications, including that

- the Old Covenant was finished.

   Luke 20:22 – *"This cup is the new covenant in my blood, which is poured out for you."*

- punishment for all sin was finished.

   Isaiah 53:5 – *...the punishment that brought us peace was upon him...*

- the law was finished.

Romans 10:4 – *Christ is the end of the law so that there may be righteousness for everyone who believes.*

- attempts at righteousness through works were finished.

Romans 11:6 – *And if [we become righteous] by grace, then **it is no longer by works**; if it were, grace would no longer be grace.* (emphasis and bracket mine)

The context of the New Covenant is grace, which means undeserved and unearned favor. **Because grace is undeserved and unearned, it is unlimited.** We can never be too undeserving to receive grace. Since Jesus obeyed the law perfectly on our behalf, we no longer have to strive to meet a standard. He already met it for us.

The eternal verdict for us who believe that Jesus is the Christ is "no condemnation."

Romans 8:1 – *Therefore, there is now no condemnation for those who are in Christ Jesus,*

Righteousness with God is accomplished by believing in what Jesus did for us and not by trying to live up to any expectation.

Unfortunately, many Christians have a hard time accepting this gift of righteousness. We still think that if we have certain sins going on in our lives then our conversion must not have been real, or that we must have fallen away. We will quote verses like

Romans 6:1-2 – *What shall we say, then? Shall we go on sinning so that grace may increase? By no means! We died to sin; how can we live in it any longer?*

in order to point out that if we live in sin, then we haven't really died to it, and therefore we must not have really become Christians. Or we think that we have fallen away or backslid in our hearts and have forfeited our salvation. This thinking is not grace-based. It is not New Covenant thinking. It is law-based, Old Covenant thinking.

This kind of thinking implies that grace has limits—that there is a line we can cross from being saved to being lost again. We will say that we are saved by grace, but we also have to keep that grace intact by how we live. If our lives don't measure up to a certain level of obedience to commands of the New or Old Testaments, then our salvation comes under question. This is combining New and Old Covenant thinking. It is mixing grace with law and, as we saw earlier, God calls this mixture the *ministry of death*.

Another Scripture that can be misunderstood or misinterpreted to think our salvation can be lost is

> **Matthew 7:21-23** – *"Not everyone who says to me, 'Lord, Lord,' will enter the kingdom of heaven, but only the one who does the will of my Father who is in heaven. Many will say to me on that day, 'Lord, Lord, did we not prophesy in your name and in your name drive out demons and in your name perform many miracles?' Then I will tell them plainly, 'I never knew you. Away from me, you evildoers!'*

There are three keys to understanding this passage. The first is that these people trusted in their works to save them. They did the same things that Jesus did but with a law-based motive, thinking that their good deeds would qualify them for salvation. They were not trusting in a Savior to rescue them; rather, trusting in their obedience to what they thought would make them good enough.

The second key is understanding what doing "the will of my Father" means. Jesus revealed what works the Father requires in the following passage...

John 6:28-29 – *They they asked him, "What must we do to do the works God requires?"*

Jesus answered, "The work of God is this: to believe in the one he has sent."

The only "work" necessary for salvation is to believe and trust in Jesus as our Lord and Savior.

The third key is where Jesus says, *"I never knew you."* The word for *knew* is the same word used to describe romantic intimacy. For example, when Mary is talking with the angel about becoming pregnant she uses this word to say that she has never known a man before. It implies becoming one with someone. We become one with Jesus when we completely trust in what He did for us on the cross and not in our own obedience.

If we think that what we do contributes to receiving or maintaining our salvation, then Jesus refers to us as *evildoers*. An evildoer, therefore, is not just someone who indulges in sin, but also someone who thinks that their obedience plays a part in their right standing with God.

In the New Covenant, grace replaces law as the only means for achieving righteousness.

> **Romans 5:20** – *...where sin increased, grace increased all the more.*

Grace is always given disproportionately to our sin. It's always more than what we need.

Grace means that any lines we could have crossed under the Old Covenant to become unrighteous have been erased. It also means that there are no new lines under the New Covenant. If there were still lines, then our salvation would really be based on our works, our deeds, our obedience, etc., and not on what Jesus did.

Grace means all of our sins have been forgiven: past, present, and future. Once we enter into the New Covenant of grace, everything we ever did or ever will do is covered by the blood of Jesus.

There are many more Scriptures that support this perspective than those that seem to contradict it. In Part III, we will look at some of these contradictory Scriptures in a new light, and view them in a way that is consistent with the finished work of the cross. **Once we understand the fact that His grace is sufficient to cover us completely, that there is no line we can cross, and that losing our salvation is impossible, then fear of rejection will no longer have a place in our relationship with God, and the power of sin in our lives will be broken.**

If any threat of losing our salvation exists, then God is manipulating us into obedience. Our motivation to pray, read the Bible, obey God, etc., will always have a root of fear (i.e. fear of rejection as opposed to being in awe of the Lord). We will always be wondering if we are measuring up or not, if we are accepted or not, if we are saved or not. There will always be a certain level of insecurity in our relationship with Him. With fear and insecurity present, we can never be at rest with Him. We will never experience *"peace that surpasses understanding"* (**Philippians 4:7**); never feel *"inexpressible joy"* (**1 Peter 1:8**); never truly trust Him; never enjoy the unbreakable, intimate connection that Jesus won for us.

Manipulation is not love, and God is love.

Unlimited grace is not a license to sin. He wants us to choose His ways because we love Him, not because we are afraid we will lose our salvation if we don't. He gives us complete freedom to choose His ways or not while having no fear of condemnation. That's what Jesus bought for us.

Without the possibility of being condemned, we can relax and enjoy Him. We can rest assured of His faithfulness. We can be confident of our permanent seat at His banquet table. We can know with certainty that He loves us just the way we are and that we don't have to change anything in order to bring

Him pleasure. Sin will lose its appeal because we will prefer His presence over interrupting our fellowship with Him.

Out of Time

Our relationship with Him has been eternally established by the blood of Jesus because the cross actually took place before time began. Nothing inside of the constraints of time can interfere with something already set in eternity. Jesus is

> **Revelation 13:8** – *...the Lamb that was slain from the creation of the world.*

This is also confirmed in what we saw with David earlier, as well as in the concept that we participated in the death, burial, and resurrection of Christ. We weren't there and yet we participated, because for God it's all outside of time. (More on this in the next chapter.)

The New Covenant can be summed up well in the following passage:

> **Ephesians 1:4-8** – *For he chose us in him before the creation of the world to be holy and blameless in his sight. In love he predestined us to be adopted as his sons through Jesus Christ, in accordance with his pleasure and will—to the praise of his glorious grace, which he has freely given us in the One he loves. In him we have redemption through his blood, the forgiveness of sins, in accordance with the riches of God's grace that he lavished on us with all wisdom and understanding.*

Let's break this passage down:

- *"he chose us"* – We didn't choose Him.

- *"before the creation of the world"* – It is outside of time, nothing can alter it.

- *"holy and blameless in his sight"* – We are perfect in God's eyes for no other reason than that we are in Jesus.

- *"In love he predestined us"* – He determined before time that we were His through love.

- *"adopted as his sons"* – Sonship is irreversible.

- *"in accordance with his pleasure"* – The fact that we are His children gives Him pleasure.

- *"his glorious grace, which he has freely given"* – Grace is a gift that is given freely and not because we do anything to qualify for it.

- *"In him we have redemption through his blood"* – We were purchased with the most valuable thing that ever existed, revealing how valuable we are to Him.

- *"the forgiveness of sins"* – Our entire debt has been wiped out.

- *"in accordance with the riches of God's grace"* – His grace for us is based on His unlimited stores of mercy.

- *"that he lavished on us"* – He gave way more than what we needed.

- *"with all wisdom and understanding"* – His plan of grace is perfect; there is no flaw in it.

There are many aspects and benefits to the New Covenant of grace. We are so blessed to live on this side of the cross, under the amazing, transforming power of unlimited grace.

Grace Glasses

Because the context of the New Covenant is grace, we must filter everything we apply to our lives from the Bible through it. We must put on "lenses of grace" so that we can see everything in the right context—even things Jesus said in the Gospels.

The writers of the Bible, after the cross, received revelation from the glorified, resurrected Christ through the Holy Spirit. What Jesus says on the resurrection side of the cross takes priority over what Jesus said on the other side because before the cross, He was still under the Old Covenant.

Again, we don't ignore what was said in the Gospels. If Jesus said it, then it's important. If He is talking about the law, we want to apply the principles of the law to our lives within the context of grace. We don't apply the standards of the law to our lives in order to qualify for salvation, and we don't apply the condemnation of the law to our lives if we don't measure up.

We must be those who are

> **2 Timothy 2:15** – ...*rightly dividing the word of truth...*

between law and grace.

In Part II, we will examine grace in greater detail so we can walk in our true identity and in the power and authority that Jesus imparts to us. In Chapter 4: Once and For All, we discover how the one event at the cross changed everything for all time.

Declarations

These statements are meant to be said out loud to God or in agreement with God—daily if possible. They are intended to solidify the gospel of grace in our hearts and minds.

- You are good, and Your love endures forever.

- You are always with me no matter where I go or what I do.

- I am perfect in Christ, so I am accepted and celebrated by You just the way I am.

- I am saved by Your grace and not by anything I do or don't do.

- The Old Covenant is dead. Grace is the new order.

PART II

GRACE AND
ALL ITS GLORY

CHAPTER 4:
ONCE AND FOR ALL

*L*et's finish this once and for all is a great line anytime there has been a long, drawn out conflict that both sides are tired of and want to be over. Sometimes it's even a fight to the death. The phrase *once and for all* means to settle a matter permanently and in a way that cannot be altered. It's short for *one time and for all time*. In other words, we are going to do something once to decide an issue and the outcome of that decision will last forever.

God's plan from before the beginning of time was for Jesus to come to earth as a man, overcome the world, keep the law perfectly His whole life, and then offer Himself as a sacrifice for the punishment for all of man's sin. When He did this, God righteously judged the sacrifice of Jesus as more than enough payment to free man from ever being condemned for any of his sin.

The problem of sin was dealt with once and for all.

Hebrews 7:27 – *He sacrificed for their sins once for all when he offered himself.*

1 Peter 3:18 – *For Christ died for sins once for all, the righteous for the unrighteous, to bring you to God.*

Punishment for our sin no longer exists. Jesus took it once and for all.

Isaiah 53:4-5 – *...he was pierced for our transgressions, he was crushed for our iniquities; the punishment that brought us peace was on him...*

Hebrews 9:12 – *With his own blood...he entered the Most Holy Place once for all time and secured our redemption forever.* (NLT)

There is no more trying to measure up to the law. Jesus measured up to it for us once and for all.

Matthew 5:17 – *(Jesus speaking) "Do not think that I have come to abolish the Law or the Prophets; I have not come to abolish them but to fulfill them."*

Galatians 3:25 – *Now that faith has come, we are no longer under the supervision of the law.*

We no longer have to work at being righteous and holy. He made us righteous and holy once and for all.

1 Corinthians 1:30 – *Jesus...has become for us...righteousness, holiness and redemption.*

2 Corinthians 5:21 – *God made him who had no sin to be sin for us, so that in him we might become the righteousness of God.*

Hebrews 10:10 – *…we have been made holy through the sacrifice of the body of Jesus Christ once for all.*

The good news is that <u>all</u> eternal punishment for <u>all</u> of man's sin was paid for on the cross, one time for all time.

(This statement can prompt the question "Then why isn't everyone automatically saved?" which we will answer in the next chapter.)

With the payment for our sin out of the way, the New Covenant of grace is made possible. It's a relationship with God where we are free to be ourselves, free to be who He made us to be, without fear of wrath or punishment for not measuring up. When we say yes to Jesus, it is once and for all.

> **Romans 8:38-39** – *For I am convinced that neither death nor life, neither angels nor demons, neither the present nor the future, nor any powers, neither height nor depth, nor anything else in all creation, will be able to separate us from the love of God that is in Christ Jesus our Lord.*

Nothing in all creation can ever separate us from Him.

One of the many amazing things about the New Covenant of grace is that He not only forgives our sins, but He also chooses to forget them. And since we would have a hard time accepting this fact, because it sounds too good to be true, He repeated it over and over.

> **Jeremiah 31:43** – *"For I will forgive their wickedness and will remember their sins no more."*

> **Hebrews 8:12** – *"For I will forgive their wickedness and will remember their sins no more."*

> **Hebrews 10:17** – *"Their sins and lawless acts I will remember no more."*

In the Hebrew (for Jeremiah) and the Greek (for Hebrews) the wording in these verses is expressed in very strong language. It means, "I will definitely not, in no way possible, remember their sins." This alone should give us a great sense of peace. When we enter the New Covenant of grace, He forgets all of our sins once and for all.

How can a holy, righteous, and just God choose to forget our sins? Has He gone soft on punishing the guilty? By no means! He forgets them because the price, penalty, and punishment for them has already been paid by Jesus. And because He is holy, righteous, and just, He cannot punish the same sin twice. If God poured out His wrath for all sin onto Jesus and then punished us for that same sin, He would not be holy, righteous, and just.

We have been declared "not guilty" in the eternal courtroom of heaven because of what Jesus has done. He confessed to our crimes. He was tried in our place. He was found guilty of all charges against us. The verdict was issued. The sentencing was set. The punishment was carried out.

In love, Jesus became guilty for all our sin and received all of our punishment so there will never, ever be any sin in our lives that we can be condemned for. IT'S GOOD NEWS!

The "In" Crowd

Back in school, there were popular kids that everyone wanted to be friends with. Most people wanted to be included in one of the "cool" groups. Some of the popular kids were good looking, some were funny, some were athletic, some were smart, some were rebels. There was an "in" crowd for almost every type of person.

We all want to feel accepted, liked, and approved of by people we admire. We all desire that they think highly of us; it helps us feel that we have value.

Whether we are part of the in crowds of the world or not, there has always been a Jesus-shaped hole in our hearts that only He can fill. And there has always been individual us-shaped holes in Jesus' heart that only we could fill.

When we go from being *in the world* to being *in Christ*, we become part of the Jesus in crowd and everything changes once and for all.

> **2 Corinthians 5:17** – ...*if anyone is in Christ, he is a new creation; the old has gone, the new has come!*

What being a new creation means is that we are no longer sinners; rather, we are an entirely new being that the earth has never seen before. In the beginning God created the heavens, the earth, the animals, and then man. But when we are born again in Jesus, God creates another new creature on the earth. We are the only living things on the planet that have God living inside of us through the Holy Spirit.

This new beginning happens when we say yes to what Jesus did for us—when we finally come to that place of surrender, that place where we are sick and tired of being lonely, frustrated, oppressed, and discouraged, and we reach out for Him. That's when the magic begins. We are miraculously transported through time and space and thrust upon the cross with Christ.

> **Galatians 2:20** – *I have been crucified with Christ and I no longer live, but Christ lives in me.*

We die with Jesus because He was not only crucified **for us,** but He was crucified **as us.** We actually participate in His death, burial, and resurrection. This is what it means to be born again. We die with Jesus, we are buried with Him, and we are raised to a new life with Him.

> **Romans 6:4** – *We were therefore buried with him through baptism into death in order that, just as Christ was raised from the dead through the glory of the Father, we too may live a new life.*

> **Colossians 2:12** – ...*having been buried with him in baptism and raised with him through your faith in the power of God, who raised him from the dead.*

Part of this spiritual renewal takes place through baptism. Baptism is a vital part of the process of being born again *in Christ*. Almost every individual conversion in the Book of Acts mentions it. Baptism plays a very important role in our conversion, which Peter sums up nicely.

> **1 Peter 3:21** – *...and this [flood] water symbolizes baptism that now saves you also--not the removal of dirt from the body but **the pledge of a good conscience toward God**. It [baptism] saves you by the resurrection of Jesus Christ...* (brackets and emphasis mine)

We know, based on other Scriptures, that it is our faith in Jesus as our Savior that grants us eternal life and not the act of being baptized. One of the theological errors that grew out of the Dark Ages was reducing salvation to merely participating in the religious ceremony of baptism. As a result, much of the modern church has overreacted to this error by watering baptism down (pun intended) to an insignificant symbolic ritual. But Peter reveals its purpose here. Baptism is where we pledge to have a good conscience toward God.

What is on our conscience? What do we mostly think about in relation to God? What motivates us? Is it His goodness, grace, and mercy? Or is it our own level of obedience and trying to live up to a standard in order to obtain acceptance?

A pledge of a good conscience does not mean we can never violate our conscience again in order to keep our salvation. It also doesn't mean we have to constantly examine ourselves and confess every sin. It means that we trust in and rely on the grace of Jesus to make us righteous and holy, not on our own good deeds or obedience.

Having a good conscience is being conscious of grace. We keep our focus on what He did for us and not on how we are doing. If we do happen to fall short in some way, we don't need to feel insecure that God is mad at us or that we have become unrighteous in His sight. Instead, we come to our heavenly Father with our hearts full of gratitude because He can never punish us with condemnation for our sins. We focus on His goodness and not on our own sinfulness.

This does not mean that there aren't consequences to us being rebellious and acting in ways that are contrary to His word and His will. There absolutely are. But no matter what the consequences may be, our salvation and righteousness are secure in Jesus.

> **Hebrews 10:22** – *let us draw near to God with a sincere heart in full assurance of faith, having our hearts sprinkled [with the blood of Christ] to cleanse us from a guilty conscience.* (brackets mine)

Many translations use *evil* instead of guilty (in this context we will use them interchangeably). An evil conscience is occupied with how we have messed up and with how we are going to try to do better so that we can once again feel confident of God's approval. It is law focused, bent on achieving a predetermined biblical standard in order to find favor with God and a sense of self-worth. It promotes a spirit of religion in that it will condemn anyone, including ourselves, who is not living up to whatever standard we feel the Bible requires of us. **Focusing on our own sinfulness is having an evil or guilty conscience,** and it distracts us from the truth of what He has accomplished for us.

This is not to say that we don't need to acknowledge and deal with our mistakes when we have messed up. We absolutely do. We also must make our best efforts to be reconciled to others when we have hurt them. Our consciences are to be led by the Holy Spirit to both clean up any messes we make and to remain aware of the grace that Jesus won for us.

The verse below contrasts animal sacrifices with Jesus' sacrifice on the cross and how they relate to our guilt. If an animal sacrifice was perfect the way Jesus' sacrifice was, then

> **Hebrews 10:2** – *...the worshipers would have been cleansed **once for all**, and would no longer have felt guilty for their sins.* (emphasis mine)

It's when we understand that God's favor and acceptance of us does not have any requirements, and that the blood of Jesus cleanses us from an evil, guilty conscience once and for all that we are free to enjoy being unconditionally welcomed into His arms, resting our heads on His bosom in complete peace and security.

The difference between these two ways of thinking makes all the difference in our relationship with God.

In response to our own mistakes or sins, the good conscience says, "Daddy, I messed up and I'm sorry. Thank You so much for Your grace and how You love me just the way I am. I am amazed by Your goodness and what You did for me on the cross. Please restore our intimate fellowship and give me greater revelations of Your love for me. Help me walk in Your ways through the power of the Holy Spirit." A good conscience fills us with joy, peace, freedom, and confidence because it is Jesus focused. This is New Covenant thinking.

Whereas the sin-focused, guilty conscience says, "God, I'm sorry I keep blowing it. I don't know why I keep doing these stupid things. I'm trying to obey the best I can and not give into temptation, but I always fall at some point. I feel like I disappoint You all the time. Please give me the strength to do better." An evil conscience fills us with insecurity, fear, doubt, and anxiety because it is self-focused. This is Old Covenant thinking.

> **Hebrews 12:1-2** – ...*let us strip off every weight that slows us down, especially the sin that so easily trips us up. And let us run with endurance the race God has set before us.* **We do this by keeping our eyes on Jesus,** *the champion who initiates and perfects our faith.* (NLT) (emphasis mine)

When we take our focus off our own performance and instead keep our eyes on Jesus, we are able to *"strip off every weight that slows us down"* and *"the sin that so easily trips us up."*

When we are baptized into Christ and we pledge to have a good conscience, the intention is to be transformed from Old Covenant thinking to New Covenant thinking. We wash away our old mindset of always examining how we are doing, and replace it with being accepted just the way we are because Jesus has made up for any and every way we will ever feel like we fall short.

Once we are in Christ, we are part of the in crowd once and for all. If we are not in Christ, then we are still in sin or in the world.

Dead and Alive

In Romans Chapter 5 through Chapter 7, the word *sin* is almost always a noun and rarely a verb. So, when it speaks of us being "dead to sin," it's not talking about the act of sinning. It's talking about sin as a person, place, or thing. One way we can look at either being in Christ or in sin is by thinking of sin as a person, just as Christ is a person. We can think of it as being under the influence or authority of that person, like we would a boss, a teacher, or a parent.

We can take it a step further and give sin a name, just like being in Christ is being in Jesus. Being in sin can be looked at as being in Satan, that is, under his influence and authority. Let's insert his name in place of the word sin and see what happens.

> **Romans 6:2** – *We are those who have died to [Satan]; how can we live under [his] influence any longer?* (change mine)

> **Romans 6:6-7** – *For we know that our old self was crucified with him [Jesus] so that the body ruled by [Satan] might be done away with, that we should no longer be slaves to [Satan]— because anyone who has died has been set free from [his] authority.* (change mine)

> **Romans 6:10-14** – *The death he [Jesus] died, he died to [Satan] once for all; but the life he lives, he lives to God. In the*

same way, count yourselves dead to [Satan] but alive to God in Christ Jesus. Therefore do not let [Satan] reign in your mortal body so that you obey [his] evil desires. Do not offer any part of yourself to [Satan] as an instrument of wickedness, but rather offer yourselves to God as those who have been brought from death to life; and offer every part of yourself to him [God] as an instrument of righteousness. For [Satan] shall no longer be your master, because you are not under the law, but under grace. (change mine)

Romans 6:18 – *You have been set free from [Satan] and have become slaves to righteousness [Jesus].* (change mine)

Because both Christ and sin are nouns, it is very helpful to use a name instead of the word *sin*, which we typically think of as a verb. It helps us to see that we are not dying to the action of sinning. When we are dead to sin, we are dead to the influence and authority that Satan once held us under. We have been set free from him and have become slaves of Jesus.

This is important because once we are dead to sin and alive to God in Christ, it is once and for all.

Romans 6:10 – *The death he died, he died to sin once for all; but the life he lives, he lives to God.*

Jesus died to sin once and for all, and because we died with Him we also died to sin once and for all. Jesus can't go back to being under the curse of sin (which happened on the cross) and, because we are in Christ, we can't go back either. He transitioned from being in sin to being in righteousness when He rose from the dead, and we moved right along with Him. Because we are in Him, His home is our home. Where He lives, we live.

Colossians 3:3 – *For you died, and your life is now hidden with Christ in God.*

Once we are in Christ, our lives are hidden in Him in eternity. But what we do and how we live still matter. Even though He knows our whole story from start to finish, we still play a crucial part in how this drama unfolds. However, we can rest assured that everything will be all right when we come to end of this life because we are already in eternity with Him.

> **Ephesians 2:6** – *And God raised us up with Christ and seated us with him in the heavenly realms in Christ Jesus...*

It's very difficult for us to wrap our minds around the fact that we are seated in the heavenly realms right now, even while we are still living and breathing on this physical planet. Our minds were programmed to think within the realm of time and space, so when we try and break out of those boundaries and into the timeless realm of eternity, our minds struggle for context.

However, once we are in Christ, we are in Him once and for all. There's no getting us out. It is one time and for all time. It is even beyond all time because the Bible says we are already in eternity with Jesus.

Plus, not only are we in Him once and for all but He is also in us once and for all. When we enter Him, He enters us as well.

> **2 Corinthians 1:22** – *[Jesus]set his seal of ownership on us, and put his Spirit in our hearts as a deposit, guaranteeing what is to come.* (brackets mine)

Jesus put the Holy Spirit inside of us and then sealed us up with His signet ring, marking us as His own. He gave us the down payment of the Holy Spirit to guarantee He will take us home when it's time. We are His; He bought us. He ransomed us from the prison of sin. After He paid the highest price possible for us, He then invested His Spirit in us to make our salvation permanent.

When He enters us and we become new creations, we are alive with a new heavenly DNA that we didn't have as pre-believers. The Holy Spirit mixes Himself into us like sweet sugar into bitter coffee. The two substances become one. Once it's in, it's in once and for all, there's no getting it out. It's the same with us and Jesus.

> **Matthew 26:26-28** – *While they were eating, Jesus took bread, gave thanks and broke it, and gave it to his disciples, saying, "Take and eat; this is my body." Then he took the cup, gave thanks and offered it to them, saying, "Drink from it, all of you. This is my blood of the covenant, which is poured out for many for the forgiveness of sins."*

When we eat the bread that represents His body and drink the cup that represents His blood, it symbolizes how our spirits feed on Him and how He is absorbed into us. When we physically eat the bread and drink the cup, the substances become one with our bodies through the digestion process. It is the same for our spirits. When we feed on the Word that came down from heaven, and when we drink in His love, He assimilates into the core of who we are. He becomes one with us.

Once we are mixed together, there is no way to un-mix us. Jesus completely alters our make-up once and for all. With Him in us, we become the fragrance of life. We go from commoner to royalty, from orphan to beloved child.

> **1 John 3:1** – *How great is the love the Father has lavished on us, that we should be called children of God! And that is what we are!*

In Jesus, God is our Father and we are His children. Once we are adopted into His family, there is nothing that can undo this relationship. **We can certainly mess up our fellowship with Him through sin, but we can never change our relationship. Relationship and fellowship are two different things.**

If my daughter is disobedient to me, it disrupts our fellowship, but it does nothing to change the fact that she is still my daughter. She could go down a very destructive path, do all sorts of things against my wishes, run away, get into a lot of trouble, and not talk to me for years; yet, she is still my daughter, born from my seed. Our fellowship can be altered but our relationship never can: once a daughter, always a daughter.

We are born again through the seed of faith planted in us by the Holy Spirit: once a child of God, always a child of God. Nothing we can do can ever change that.

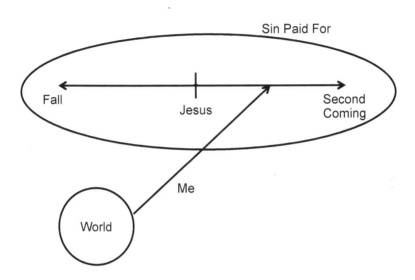

Let's get a piece of paper and a pencil and make a timeline starting with the fall of Adam and Eve and ending with the Second Coming. Draw a horizontal line and write *Fall* on the left end and *Second Coming* on the right. Now let's put a mark in the middle of the line and write *Jesus* to represent when He died, was buried, and was raised again. Because of Jesus' death, burial, and resurrection, let's draw an oval around the entire timeline to show that Jesus paid for all sin, for all people, for all time. On top of the oval write *Sin Paid For*. Now, draw a circle below the oval and label it *World*. Make an arrow going from the world to someplace between *Jesus* and *Second Coming* to show when you came out of the world and became a Christian. Write *Me* next to the arrow.

This shows that in order for people in the world to be included in what Jesus has already done for them, they simply need to believe it. Once we are included in *Sin Paid For*, there isn't any sin we could commit in our lifetime that is not already paid for. It is our gratitude for this amazing grace that woos us into loving Him and compels us to live as He wants.

"Oh, You Mean Daddy!"

A friend of mine has a ministry where she sets up a booth at different street fairs around our area and gives away free encouraging words from God. People come into the tent and sit down. Two or three of us will be there with them and we will quiet ourselves and listen in our spirit to what God wants to tell them. I start writing what I hear because it seems to flow better for me, but others see pictures and draw them or just repeat what they hear the Spirit saying.

Many times the people are a little worried that we are going to tell them negative things about how they are messing up, but that's not God's heart for us. It's always good—always positive—and people are blown away by how accurate we are with what they are going through in their lives and by how encouraging the words are. Many times they are so touched they are brought to tears. They can feel His love for them, and they just want to stay there in His presence.

We also interpret dreams or tattoos through the Holy Spirit. They have spiritual meanings and when we tell people what the meanings are, their faces just light up.

One time a young man with Down's syndrome came in and asked us to interpret a dream for him. He described the dream as having green grass, butterflies, trees, puppies, and a waterfall. One of us said that it sounded like a picture of heaven where the Creator lives. (We try to use non-religious language because we don't know people's backgrounds.) He smiled really wide and said, "Yeah, I go there a lot." We asked if he knew who the Creator was. He thought for a second and then a light seemed to come on: "Oh, you mean Daddy!" We all laughed and one of us said, "Maybe you should be ministering to us!"

> **Romans 8:15-16** – *For you did not receive a spirit that makes you a slave again to fear, but you received the Spirit of sonship. And by him we cry, "Abba, Father." The Spirit himself testifies with our spirit that we are God's children.*

Abba is a Hebrew word for father but in the most affectionate and intimate sense. For us it would be similar to "Da-da" or "Daddy." Unfortunately, many Christians are uncomfortable calling Him by such an informal, familiar term, as if they are afraid of offending Him or being irreverent. But that's not His concern. He wants us to feel safe and secure in His unfailing love and His total acceptance of us to the point where we can call Him *Daddy* and enjoy His "warm fuzzies from heaven."

His heart for us is so tender and kind. He is so warm and gentle. He just loves it when we curl up in His lap and let Him wrap His arms around us. It's a beautiful moment when we can rest in His presence and enjoy Him enjoying us. He is a good Daddy who is full of affection for us. (Read *Always Loved* by Pastor Brent Lokker.)

If we are insecure with Him then we are not in step with the Holy Spirit and we are not confident of what it means to be His child. We sons and daughters should not be afraid of our Daddy. If we are, then we have more of a slave mentality than that of a beloved son or daughter. Slaves are afraid of not pleasing their master and work very hard at trying to do everything right, so they don't get in trouble. Sons and daughters, on the other hand, are secure in their position in the family and serve out of knowing how much they are valued.

> **John 8:35** – *(Jesus speaking) "Now a slave has no permanent place in the family, but a son belongs to it forever."*

When we become His children, it is permanent, and it is forever. It is once and for all!

In Chapter 5, the mystery of the unforgivable sin is unveiled.

Declarations

- All my sins—past, present, and future—are already paid for. You have forgotten them.

- You have declared me innocent because there is no evidence against me.

- Because I am one with You, Jesus, I am perfectly righteous, completely holy, a saint; I am prone to righteousness, I am not prone to sin; I am a new creature, the old one is gone, the new has come!

- I am seated with You, Jesus, in the heavenly places far above all rule, power, authority, and above every name that is named, not only in this age, but also the age to come!

- I am Your child, and You are my Father. Nothing can ever change that. It's once and for all.

CHAPTER 5:
THE UNFORGIVABLE SIN

Many of us have a line. We might not know it or even know where it is, but we have one. It's a line that sets a hard boundary against someone violating us in some way. If someone crosses that line, it will be extremely difficult, if not impossible, to forgive that person.

Some of us have already had this line crossed. Maybe we had an abusive parent that we cannot forgive. Maybe someone murdered a loved one. Maybe our spouse committed adultery. Maybe our business partner cheated us. Whatever it is, we can find ourselves in a situation where we cannot bring ourselves to forgive this person for the hurt they have caused us. We might even *want* to forgive them because God has forgiven us, but we just can't seem to get there.

We can try to forgive the best we can, but only God forgives people completely. The Bible says that the sins of the entire world were forgiven on the cross, not just the sins of those who believe in Jesus. Everyone's.

> **John 1:29** – *(John the Baptist speaking of Jesus) "...the Lamb of God, who takes away **the sin of the world!**"*

John 3:17 – *For God did not send his Son into the world to condemn the world, but **to save the world** through him.*

John 6:51 – *(Jesus speaking) "This bread is my flesh, which I will give for **the life of the world**."*

2 Corinthians 5:19 – *God was **reconciling the world** to himself in Christ, not counting men's sins against them.*

1 John 2:2 – *He is the atoning sacrifice for our sins, and **not only for ours but also for the sins of the whole world**.*

1 John 4:14 – *...the Father has sent his Son to be the **Savior of the world**.*

(brackets and emphasis mine)

- At the cross, all sins for all people were forgiven. It doesn't matter if someone is Hindu, Muslim, Buddhist, Atheist, or Christian, Jesus' blood washed away all the sin of the entire world: everyone who has ever lived or whoever will live was cleansed at that moment.

Now, remember the question from the last chapter? "If the cross pays for all sin, then why isn't everyone automatically saved?" We will let Jesus answer that one.

Mark 3:28-29 – *"I tell you the truth, all the sins and blasphemies of men will be forgiven them. But whoever blasphemes against the Holy Spirit will never be forgiven; he is guilty of an eternal sin."*

Jesus confirms here that all sins would be forgiven at the cross; however, He also indicates that there's **only one sin** that wouldn't be instantly forgiven, and that's blaspheming the Holy Spirit. This is the unforgivable sin.

But what does it mean to blaspheme the Holy Spirit? *Blaspheme* is not a word that we use in our culture. It means "to bitterly complain against," "to speak evil of," or "to slander."[6]

In the verses immediately before this, some religious leaders were accusing Jesus of healing people and driving out demons with satanic powers and not with the Holy Spirit. Jesus essentially told them that Satan is not divided against himself, and that it was by the Spirit of God that He was doing these things.

Some teach that blaspheming the Holy Spirit is doing what these religious leaders did, that it is giving credit to Satan for something that was really done by the Holy Spirit. If this were true, anyone could mistakenly commit this sin and immediately lose their salvation permanently. Or they could be disqualified from ever being saved in the first place. However, this point of view does not line up with the heart of grace we see in Jesus, nor with the grace we see in other passages already mentioned.

For example, Paul was a Pharisee who persecuted the church so intensely before his conversion that he gave approval for Christians to be killed. He did this out of an intense, although misguided, desire to serve God. Surely he didn't think the miracles being done through the Christians of his day were powered by the Holy Spirit. It's likely that he agreed with the accusations of the other religious leaders that these signs were due to satanic influences and were done by the hand of God. Clearly he was not guilty of "an eternal sin" as he went on to become one of the most powerful leaders in the church, writing two-thirds of the New Testament.

There are also many Christian churches today that believe the miraculous signs and wonders we read about in the Bible died out with the apostles. While some of them would attribute some of today's miracles to God, others would not, misusing passages like this one:

2 Thessalonians 2:9-12 – *The coming of the lawless one will be in accordance with how Satan works. He will use all sorts of* *displays of power through signs and wonders that serve the lie, and all the ways that wickedness deceives those who are perishing. They perish because they refused to love the truth and so be saved. For this reason God sends them a powerful delusion so that they will believe the lie and so that all will be condemned who have not believed the truth but have delighted in wickedness.*

Many Christians judge today's miracles, signs, and wonders with this passage out of fear of being deceived. They claim that these miracles are a powerful delusion that God is allowing Satan to display to people who are not really Christians.

In Matthew's account regarding blaspheming the Holy Spirit, Jesus goes on to say that we will know a tree by its fruit. The vast majority of the miraculous signs happening today are taking place in and through people who profess Jesus as Lord, who love to worship Him, and who attempt to live according to the principles in the Scriptures. They are upstanding believers with good fruit, and they see amazing things through the power of the Holy Spirit.

Are the Christians who judge these miracles as a being from the enemy going to hell because they are blaspheming the Holy Spirit? Again, this view isn't consistent with other passages we see on grace.

In order for us to understand how someone can bitterly complain against the Holy Spirit, we must first look at what the Holy Spirit's role is here on earth.

Paul preaches:

1 Corinthians 2:13 – *...in words taught by the Spirit...*

Peter says that others have

1 Peter 1:12 – *...preached the gospel to you by the Holy Spirit sent from heaven.*

Other Scriptures also mention different ways the Spirit works.

1 Corinthians 12:3 – *...no one can say, "Jesus is Lord," except by the Holy Spirit.*

Ephesians 2:18 – *Now all of us can come to the Father through the same Holy Spirit because of what Christ has done for us.*

2 Thessalonians 2:13 – *...from the beginning God chose you to be saved through the sanctifying work of the Spirit...*

One of the Holy Spirit's main purposes is to constantly work in people's lives through all sorts of means to get everyone to accept the gift of salvation that Jesus purchased at the cross. It is also the Holy Spirit who works in believers to lead, counsel, reveal truth, give miraculous gifts, and bear fruits of the Spirit, all for the purpose of leading everyone in the world to Christ. The Holy Spirit is the great evangelist.

John 16:8-11 – *(Jesus speaking about the Holy Spirit) "When he comes, he will convict the world of guilt in regard to sin and righteousness and judgment: in regard to sin, because men do not believe in me; in regard to righteousness, because I am going to the Father, where you can see me no longer; and in regard to judgment, because the prince of this world now stands condemned."* (brackets mine)

Notice that the Holy Spirit convicts the **world** in regard to sin, righteousness, and judgment. Not Christians. And what is the **one sin** that the Holy Spirit convicts the world of? Not believing in Jesus (v. 9). It's the only sin that wasn't already paid for at the cross and the one sin that excludes those in the world from salvation.

In Acts 7, Stephen talks to the religious leaders about Jesus. Near the end of his speech, he uses a word other than *blaspheme* in the same context that

Jesus was speaking about. It is translated "resist" and it refers to people who refuse to accept Jesus as the Christ. He says...

Acts 7:51 – *"...you always resist the Holy Spirit..."*

This word also means "to strive against," "to be adverse," and "to oppose."[7]

Typically when we are adverse to something and we oppose it, we can't help but voice our displeasure about it. What we say is more powerful than we sometimes realize. With words we can build up or we can tear down. Our words can bring life or death (**Proverbs 18:21**). It was with words that God created the universe. He spoke it into existence.

At the end of the passage where Jesus is talking about blaspheming the Holy Spirit, again in Matthew's account, He says,

Matthew 12:37 – *"For by your words you will be acquitted, and by your words you will be condemned."*

Is Jesus telling us that we have to watch every single word we say because if we say the wrong thing, it will condemn us? Remember, context is everything. He is talking to religious leaders who are accusing Him of being partners with Satan. He's not speaking to or about New Covenant believers, who have already been acquitted (declared not guilty) because the Holy Spirit prompted us to say the words "Jesus is Lord!" He was addressing those who didn't have faith that He was the Messiah.

God repeated multiple times that He would absolutely not, in no way possible, remember our sins. Similarly, He tells us over and over that our words will either acquit us or condemn us.

Joel 2:32 – *...everyone who calls on the name of the Lord will be saved.*

Acts 2:21 - *"...everyone who calls on the name of the Lord will be saved."*

> **Romans 10:13** – *"...everyone who calls on the name of the Lord will be saved."*

Only those who refuse to call on the name of the Lord will be condemned. This refusal is blasphemous to all the efforts the Holy Spirit has made over the person's life to bring them to Jesus. More than likely, they have said things at different times that show their opposition to Jesus. Maybe it was as innocent as, "I have no interest in religion," or maybe it was as blatant as, "Jesus is a fairy tale and anyone who believes in Him is an idiot." These are words that slander and speak evil against the Holy Spirit's work in their lives.

The Holy Spirit is always wooing us, drawing us, enticing us to come home, to come back to our Daddy so our souls can be at rest in the security of His tender mercies.

For God

> **John 3:16** – *...so loved the world that he gave his one and only Son, that whoever believes in him shall not perish but have eternal life.*

> **1 Timothy 2:4** – *...wants all people to be saved and to come to a knowledge of the truth.*

> **2 Peter 3:9** – *...is patient with you, not wanting anyone to perish, but everyone to come to repentance.*

Because His love is unfailing and His mercy endures forever, the Holy Spirit will not stop pursuing us, so we shouldn't give up on anyone either.

The bottom line is this: if, by the time we die, we have not made Jesus our Lord and Savior, then we have resisted, opposed, and bitterly complained against the Holy Spirit's efforts to save us—we have blasphemed the Holy Spirit. Refusing to become a Christian is the only sin that will prevent us from being saved. Murder, adultery, hatred, greed, etc. won't. Those have already been paid for on the cross.

The Scriptures are not clear as to what awaits those who pass away without ever having the chance to consciously choose to accept or reject Jesus. Given God's extravagant heart of love and grace that He displayed on the cross, we can be confident that everyone will be given a fair and just opportunity to choose.

If we have accepted Jesus as our Lord and Savior, we can never blaspheme the Holy Spirit. That possibility has been removed from our lives. For a Christian, there is no unforgivable sin. We can relax and enjoy the complete security of our salvation, letting our peace and joy overflow to others.

In Chapter 6, we will find out how God has done everything for us and how all we need to do is receive it.

Declarations

- Heavenly Father, You are a good Daddy, and I eagerly anticipate seeing Your goodness today.

- Jesus, You are my Lord and Savior. I am totally surrendered to all of Your plans for me.

- Holy Spirit, please lead me in everything I do, and do not let me be led by my soul (mind, will, and emotions) or the cravings of my body.

CHAPTER 6:
I HAD NOTHING TO DO WITH IT

I became a Christian in 1989 during my last semester of college. It was in a church where we had to live up to what we thought the Bible said a real disciple of Jesus was in order to qualify for and maintain our salvation. We were unknowingly law-based, but we believed we were truly obeying the Scriptures whereas most everyone else who called themselves Christians were not.

When I was going through the lengthy series of Bible studies to be converted I remember getting angry at God. "Why is it that I'm going to hell when I was made this way? I have no chance of making it to heaven because I have a sinful nature. I can't help but fall short. How is this fair?!" I felt falsely accused and, as it turns out, I was right.

> **Romans 5:17-21** – *For if, by the trespass of the one man [Adam], death reigned through that one man, how much more will those who receive God's abundant provision of grace and of the gift of righteousness reign in life through the one man, Jesus Christ.*

*Consequently, just as **the result of one trespass was condemnation for all men**, so also **the result of one act of righteousness was justification that brings life for all men**. For just as through the disobedience of the one man the many were made sinners, so also through the obedience of the one man the many will be made righteous. The law was added so that the trespass might increase. But where sin increased, grace increased all the more, so that, just as sin reigned in death, so also grace might reign through righteousness to bring eternal life through Jesus Christ our Lord.*

(brackets and emphasis mine)

We were made sinners by Adam's disobedience and not because we sinned. It was his trespass that condemned us. Thanks to Adam, we stood sentenced to hell without any chance of redemption no matter how well we obeyed or how many good things we did. I shouldn't have been mad at God, I should have been mad at Adam. (This is not to say we are completely innocent in the matter. We would have done the same thing Adam did. Plus, we have all willfully sinned many times over.)

Because our Father is perfectly just He couldn't leave us in this no-win situation. We had nothing to do with why we were lost so, in His righteousness, He provided a rescue for us that also had nothing to do with us. **If condemnation came from being born into the inheritance of Adam's sin, then salvation would come by being born again into the inheritance of Jesus' righteousness.**

Physically, we do nothing to be born. We are just there. Everything is being done to us and for us because we are unable to contribute anything to help. What is happening is beyond our ability and understanding. We are helpless, powerless, and incapable to provide any assistance in the process.

In the same way, when we are born again, it is all done to us and for us by Jesus. We are helpless to contribute anything because what is required is beyond our capabilities. The process we need to go through in order to become righteous is out of reach of anything we could do. We can't help at all. Perfection is necessary and anything we can do just isn't good enough, so God did it all for us.

We had nothing to do with getting lost, so it's only fair and just that we have nothing to do with getting saved.

What does verse 17 say about how we get grace? We *"receive God's abundant provision of grace."* It is nothing we do. We simply receive the gift of grace, and this grace we receive doesn't just barely cover us. It isn't fragile or in short supply. An "abundant provision" is too much for what is needed. It's overflowing. It's way more than what is necessary to do the job. So much so that it didn't just pay a little more than what we owed but a lot more than what we could ever possibly owe.

Out-sinning God's abundant provision of grace is impossible because all sin for all time was already paid for. Grace is infinite; we are finite. Grace is perfect; we are imperfect. Grace is eternal; we are temporal (in this body). Infinite always triumphs over finite. Perfect always triumphs over imperfect. Eternal always triumphs over temporal. Grace is way too powerful for our sin to even make a dent in it. Our sins are a grain of sand and grace is an ocean.

> **1 Corinthians 15:54** – *"Death [sin] has been swallowed up in victory [grace]."*

(brackets mine)

Righteous, Dude

Not only do we receive more than enough grace to swallow up all our sins, but we also receive *"the gift of righteousness"* at the same time. The only requirement to receive a gift is being willing. Many of us don't feel worthy enough to receive gifts, especially such an extravagant gift from God. But that false humility will prevent us from experiencing the peace and joy that come from the love He desires to lavish on us. We are worthy because He said so, and He said so by sending Jesus. Who are we to argue with God?

God gave us the law so that we would sin more. Yes, that's what Romans 5:20 says. But where we sinned more, God gave even more grace because that's how grace works. It is always given in a greater amount than the punishment the offense deserves.

In verse 21 it says that sin (i.e. Satan) used to rule over us when we were spiritually dead. When we were born again, grace took over as our king. Grace has become our master, our leader, our covering, and this grace leads us into eternal life through Jesus.

Let's take a look at an alternate version of this passage to enhance our understanding of it.

> **Romans 5:17-21** – *By the sin of Adam, spiritual and physical death was made king. But now, we have been made kings to a greater degree because we have received more than enough grace and the gift of being acceptable to God through what Jesus did. Through Adam's sin all men were condemned but through Jesus' righteousness God declared all men to be free from guilt and acceptable to Him. By Adam's disobedience we became devoted to sin, but through Jesus' obedience we became innocent, faultless, approved by God. The Law was given so that sin would superabound; where sin was overly abundant, grace was beyond measure, so that, just as sin became king in death, grace is now king through the righteousness of Jesus for everlasting life.*

One of the most amazing things about the gift of righteousness that He gives us is that He gives us **His righteousness.** It is His righteousness that is credited to us and it does not come from our obedience. He gives us what He has to give and what He has is perfect righteousness.

> **Romans 1:17** – *For in the gospel a **righteousness from God** is revealed, a righteousness that is by faith from first to last, just as it is written: "The righteous will live by faith."*

Romans 3:21-22 – *But now a **righteousness from God**, apart from law, has been made known, to which the Law and the Prophets testify. This **righteousness from God** comes through faith in Jesus Christ to all who believe.*

Philippians 3:9 – *...**not having a righteousness of my own** that comes from the law [obedience], but that which is through faith in Christ—the **righteousness that comes from God** and is by faith.*

2 Corinthians 5:21 – *God made him who had no sin to be sin for us, so that **in him we might become the righteousness of God**.*

(emphasis and brackets mine)

God gave us His own righteousness through our faith in Jesus. We had nothing to do with becoming righteous. It was a gift. Because it is His righteousness, not ours, we can't mess it up. **How could little people trapped momentarily in time ever do anything to damage the righteousness of the all-knowing, all-powerful, ever-present, ever-perfect, eternal Creator of life?** It's foolish and arrogant to think we have that kind of power.

If our righteousness was based on our obedience, then we would not be saved by grace and Jesus died in vain.

Galatians 2:21 – *...if righteousness could be gained through the law [obedience], Christ died for nothing!* (bracket mine)

The law is all about living up to a standard in order to be righteous or to qualify for salvation. Grace is all about Jesus being righteous for us so that once we receive His gift of righteousness, we will be empowered to *"go and sin no more."*

And what does God say about His gifts?

Romans 11:29 – *God's gifts...are irrevocable.*

Once He gives us the gift of His righteousness, He can't take it back. We can't return it. We can't give it away. We can't throw it away. Why? Because it's not our righteousness. It's His.

He credits our account with it once and for all and we had nothing to do with it, except to say, "Yes, I believe that Jesus died for me, and I receive Him as my Lord and Savior," or something similar to that.

If we had to do anything more than just receive it, we would be attempting to earn our own righteousness. Anytime we have to do anything to qualify for something, then we are working to deserve it.

> **Romans 4:4-5** – *Now to the one who works, wages are not credited as a gift but as an obligation. However, to the one who does not work but trusts God who justifies the ungodly, their faith is credited as righteousness.*

God justifies the *"ungodly"* by faith, not those who work at their own righteousness. The righteousness we attempt to work for will always fall short because perfect righteousness is required to fulfill the law and to qualify for salvation. He gives us His perfect righteousness because we are ungodly, so all we can do is trust Him to justify us.

If we have to "repent of our sins" in order to qualify for salvation, we are working to obtain our own righteousness. We are trying to live up to a certain expectation that we think the Bible requires, so we can then receive and hold onto the promise of eternal life. But if we had to do this, we would be constantly examining ourselves the rest of our lives so we could continually attempt to overcome our shortcomings and thereby keep our salvation. It creates a treadmill of striving to obey in order to prove we are meeting the requirements. This is man-focused, law-based thinking and comes from works-oriented, human wisdom. (More on repentance later in this chapter.)

In the New Testament, when God talks about salvation as a gift, He chooses to use a unique word, *charisma*, to describe it. Charisma means "a free gift of grace." Different words are used to describe other types of gifts in the Bible, such as bringing a gift to the altar. But charisma is not associated with anything other than undeserved and unearned favor. Once someone tries to do something to qualify for it, it is no longer undeserved or unearned, it is no longer charisma.

> **Romans 5:15-16** – *But the **gift** is not like the trespass. For if the many died by the trespass of the one man, how much more did God's grace and the **gift** that came by the grace of the one man, Jesus Christ, overflow to the many! Nor can the **gift** of God be compared with the result of one man's sin: The judgment followed one sin and brought condemnation, but the **gift** followed many trespasses and brought justification.*

> **Romans 6:23** – *For the wages of sin is death, but the **gift** of God is eternal life in Christ Jesus our Lord.*

(all emphasis mine)

The words used for *gift* in these passages, referring to our salvation and justification through Jesus, are charisma words. Salvation is a gift, righteousness is a gift, justification is a gift, the Holy Spirit is a gift: all undeserved and unearned. Once God gives a gift, it is impossible for Him to take it away; it's once and for all. And, because it's a gift, we had nothing to do with it.

Faith, Faith, Faith

The purpose of grace is to supply life, and the purpose of faith is to receive it. But do we have enough faith to receive these free gifts of grace? Where does this faith come from?

> **Romans 10:17** – *Consequently, faith comes from hearing the message, and the message is heard through the word of Christ.*

One way faith comes to us is when we hear the message of the grace of Jesus.

The more we hear about what He did for us, the more we believe in how much He loves us, who He says we are, who He made us to be, and what He wants us to do. The word *hearing* in this verse is perpetual. It means that faith comes from hearing about what Jesus did for us again and again. The more we inundate ourselves with this message of grace, the more our faith grows. We should completely immerse ourselves in it so that we can radiate it to others. When we stop hearing the message of Jesus, our faith begins to decrease as does our impact on those around us.

Faith does not come from hearing message after message on how we are falling short in some area of our lives and how we need to repent and get right with God. These messages make us focus on ourselves instead of on Jesus. They give us a guilty conscience and burden us with demands of the law. They attempt to use duty and obligation as motivation instead of having us be compelled by the gift of grace—the everlasting love we freely receive from Him. We can only freely give what we've freely received.

Some of us who are more law focused will question the salvation of others because we disagree with how they are living. In doing so, we are really questioning whether God gave them enough faith to be saved. Instead of celebrating the work that God has done and continues to do in them, we judge that what He has done is not good enough.

Everyone falls short in some way. Engaging in an activity or lifestyle that is unbiblical does not mean a person is lost. This is Old Covenant, law-based thinking that promotes the spirit of religion. It breeds condemnation, accusation, judgment, self-righteousness, pride, etc.

Romans 14:4 – *Who are you to judge someone else's servant?*

The master (Jesus) will help us (His servants) overcome whatever challenges or weaknesses are causing us to stumble. We need to give grace to each other like He gives grace to us. None of us have "arrived." No one is perfect. Therefore, we cannot judge if someone is lost or saved. We can only attempt to love and encourage everyone in their unique journey, trusting God to help them overcome.

The more messages of grace we hear, and the more we encounter His unconditional love both directly and through other believers, the more we will believe in what Jesus did for us, the more grace we are able to extend to others, and the more motivated we are to live in a way that honors Him. (More on obedience in Chapter 8.)

Faith is believing in something that we have no proof of, yet we know in our heart, soul, and spirit that it is true because this faith comes from the One who made us.

> **2 Peter 1:1** – *This faith was given to you because of the justice and fairness of Jesus Christ, our God and Savior.* (NLT)

Faith was given to us because Jesus is just and fair. It wasn't our fault we were lost, so in God's fairness and justice, He not only gave us Jesus to pay the price for us, but He also gave us the faith we needed to believe in Him so we could be saved through Him. That's why it's good news. God did it all for us; we had nothing to do with it.

A Change of Mind

According to Scripture, there are two things required in order for us to be saved: faith and repentance. If He gives us the faith we need to be saved, it's a safe bet that He will give us the repentance, too.

There's a common misconception that repentance means to confess our sins, stop doing them, and turn to God. These things are actually the results of repentance. This definition is one that evolved through the ages right along with religion and all of its wandering from correct theology.

The true meaning of the word *repent* means to "change one's mind." Yes, it's that simple. Anything more has been incorrectly added. The Greek word is *metanoia*. *Meta* means "to change" and *noia* means "mind" or "thinking."

There can be many reasons for having a change of mind and many different emotions involved as well. Repentance can happen from inspiration just as easily as it can from regret. The important thing is allowing God to align our thinking with His.

> **Acts 2:38** – *Peter replied, "Repent and be baptized, every one of you, in the name of Jesus Christ for the forgiveness of your sins. And you will receive the gift of the Holy Spirit."*

Peter said this after the Holy Spirit came with such incredible power that the Christians appeared to be drunk. When he told them that they (the Jews) killed the Messiah, they asked him what they should do. He said they need to change their minds and be baptized.

What did these Jews need to change their minds about? The same thing that everyone who is lost needs to change his or her mind about. It is the revelation that Jesus is the Son of God, He died for our sins, and then rose from the dead on the third day. As we have already seen, every other sin has already been paid for. When God gives us this revelation of Jesus, it usually comes packaged with the faith to take action. On that day, 3,000 people were hit with this mind-changing, faith-giving experience.

Revelation causes repentance because it changes how we think about something. **True biblical repentance, as it relates to getting saved, is simply changing our minds about who Jesus is and receiving Him as Lord and Savior.** It is not about our sin; it's not even about us. It's all about Him. This change of mind happens as the result of all the work the Holy Spirit has been doing in our lives. He coordinates events and people in our lives at just the right times to bring us to the point where we are ripe to see our need for Jesus, get the revelation about who He is, and receive the faith to surrender our lives to Him. There are a lot of moving pieces and the Holy Spirit is brilliant in doing just the right thing at just the right time.

> **Acts 5:31** – *God exalted him [Jesus] to his own right hand as Prince and Savior that **he might bring Israel to repentance** and forgive their sins.*

> **Acts 11:18** – *"So then, even to Gentiles **God has granted repentance** that leads to life."*

(brackets and emphasis mine)

The same Greek word is used for *bring* to repentance in Acts 5 and *granted* repentance in Acts 11. It means "to give, of one's own accord and with good will."[8] **Repentance is something given to us by God out of His desire to have us be united with Him.** He takes away the veil at the right time (**2 Corinthians 3:16**) and changes our minds with the revelation of Jesus, just like He did with Peter in the following passage.

> **Matthew 16:15-17** – *"But what about you?" [Jesus] asked. "Who do you say I am?"*

> *Simon Peter answered, "You are the Messiah, the Son of the living God."*

> *Jesus replied, "Blessed are you, Simon son of Jonah, for **this was** not **revealed** to you by flesh and blood, but **by my Father in heaven**.*

(brackets and emphasis mine)

Jesus called Peter *blessed* because our Father revealed the truth to him about who Jesus was. When God changes our minds with the revelation of who Jesus is, it is the biggest blessing we can ever receive. It all comes from Him as a gift—a blessing given out of His uncontainable kindness to us.

> **Romans 2:4** – *God's kindness is intended to **lead you to repentance*** (emphasis mine)

The expanded definition for *lead* here is "to lead along, take with oneself, to lead towards a point." [9] God takes us by the hand and leads us to the point where the real Jesus becomes real to us—the point where we surrender to His Lordship. Then He can let go of our hand and take up residence inside us, becoming one with us forever. Our only contribution to repenting is letting Him lead us. Our only action to getting saved is receiving the gift. All we have to do is say yes to Him.

> **Luke 15:3-7** *Then Jesus told them this parable:"Suppose one of you has a hundred sheep and loses one of them. Doesn't he leave the ninety-nine in the open country and go after the lost sheep until he finds it? And when he finds it, he joyfully puts it on his shoulders and goes home. Then he calls his friends and neighbors together and says, 'Rejoice with me; I have found my lost sheep.' I tell you that in the same way there will be more rejoicing in heaven over one sinner who repents than over ninety-nine righteous persons who do not need to repent."*

Jesus compares us to this lost sheep and implies that we need to repent like this sheep did. So what did the sheep do to repent? He let himself be found, let himself be picked up, and let himself be taken home. That's it. What does the shepherd (i.e. Jesus) do? He goes after the lost sheep, finds it, joyfully puts it on His shoulders, carries it home, calls His friends and neighbors, and rejoices.

It's possible the sheep was feeling a lot of things when the shepherd found him. He could have been scared, sorry he wandered away, or even oblivious to the fact he was lost. But the one critical thing the sheep did was allow the shepherd to save him.

Jesus says that we need to repent in the same way as this sheep. We must let Him come after us, find us, put us on His shoulders, and carry us home. We simply must let Him save us. When we do that, Jesus and all His buddies in heaven have a party for us!

Immediately after this parable, Jesus goes on to teach two more parables on the same subject of repentance. He speaks about a lost coin and, again, how we need to repent by letting ourselves be found (**Luke 15:8-10**). Then He tells the famous parable of The Lost (or Prodigal) Son (**Luke 15:11-32**), but He doesn't directly mention repentance in this story. Instead, He uses this story as a practical example of the two parables that He just told, showing us exactly how repentance works in real life.

> **Luke 15:17-20** – *"When he came to his senses, he said, 'How many of my father's hired servants have food to spare, and here I am starving to death! I will set out and go back to my father and say to him: Father, I have sinned against heaven and against you. I am no longer worthy to be called your son; make me like one of your hired servants.' So he got up and went to his father."*

It appears that the son came to repentance all on his own and changed his own mind about what he was doing and the direction his life was heading. But the two parables before this show us that something else is actually happening. *"When he came to his senses"* is when he let Jesus find him and give him the gift of repentance (i.e. a change of mind). The phrase is most often translated, *"When he came to himself,"* meaning that he had previously abandoned his true identity as a son of the king but now his mind had been renewed back to right thinking. This is where he finally allowed the voice of God, which always speaks truth, to lead him to repentance. In essence, **repentance is where we let God change our thinking so that it agrees with His.**

The son let Jesus find him, pick him up, and carry him home. Then they called all their friends and had a party. It's possible the son was feeling sorry he ever left home and wasted his inheritance indulging in sin. It's also possible he was just really hungry. The reason we let God change our minds doesn't matter. All that matters is that we let Him.

Once we allow God to save us, there will almost always be things in our lives that are not consistent with His plans for us. As we let Him, He will continue to change our minds so that we can be in step with His desires and know

Him in deeper ways. Every time we read our Bibles or listen to a message about Jesus, we are repenting; He is changing our minds, giving us more revelation of who He is, and highlighting things, so we can draw closer to Him or overcome some kind of challenge. Every time we open our hearts to worship Him or experience His presence, He is changing our minds in some way to think more like Him, to know more of who He made us to be and what He wants us to do.

> **2 Corinthians 7:10** – *Godly sorrow brings repentance that leads to salvation and leaves no regret, but worldly sorrow brings death.*

Some have taken this Scripture out of context to mean that in order for us to repent and be saved we first need to have *"godly sorrow"* because it *"leads to salvation."* The context of this verse is in reference to Paul's previous letter to the Corinthian church about a believer who was having an inappropriate relationship with his step-mother. This brother was already saved, so godly sorrow couldn't be leading him to be saved again.

Rather, **godly sorrow will bring a change to our way of thinking that will lead us to experience our salvation in the way God intended,** in a way that brings life to us. If we only have worldly sorrow, we will continue to do more spiritual damage to ourselves and others. Since it is impossible for us to lose our salvation, *"death"* in this verse does not mean that we will be lost if we only have worldly sorrow. The word has other implications. Another way we could write this verse so that it does not lead us to incorrect doctrinal conclusions is something like, "Godly sorrow brings a change of mind that leads to an abundant life without regret, but worldly sorrow brings misery to the soul."

Godly sorrow is where we allow the Holy Spirit to convict us of our righteousness in Christ. He lets us know that what we are doing is not the way a prince or princess of the kingdom should live. He calls us back up to the higher place of living—a place above the law, above the flesh, where grace rules, and where we walk in its power and authority.

Worldly sorrow is where we grieve the Holy Spirit and make excuses, rationalizations, and justifications for our sinful actions. We blame others or believe a lie that what we are doing is necessary for us to be happy. We think we can't live without whatever it is even though it's taking us further from God and others. It is bringing death to our souls (i.e. our mind, will, and emotions), yet we refuse to let go of it.

Like the faith we need to be saved, repentance is also a gift from Him that we have nothing to do with. We simply must allow Him to give it to us. It just takes willingness on our part.

It's a Set-Up

A 35-year-old man bought a used pick-up truck. When he turned on the radio, the only station that he could tune in was a Christian station. This is miraculous in and of itself simply because most commercial radio stations have much stronger transmitters than the donation-based Christian stations. This man wasn't a Christian but, since it was the only station he could get, he started listening to it. After a while, the songs ministered to him and helped him change his mind about Jesus. It wasn't long afterwards that he decided to give his life to Christ.

This wasn't an accident or a coincidence. It was a divine set-up. That's just what the Holy Spirit does. He relentlessly pursues us. He will wear us down to the point where we are finally ready to give up on trying to fill the God-shaped hole in our hearts with everything but Him. Anything the world has to offer will keep getting less and less satisfying. Eventually, we get to the end of ourselves where we feel the only choice we have is to "come to our senses" and let Him bring us home.

It's all from Him. We have nothing to do with it, except to say yes to the gift of Jesus when He has led us to the point of surrender.

Chapter 7: Breaking the Law, looks at how the devil uses the law to gain power over us...if we let him.

Declarations

- I eagerly receive all the gifts You have for me.

- You received my sin on the cross, and I received Your righteousness when I believed.

- I am completely surrendered to all Your plans for me.

- You renew my mind so that I have the mind of Christ.

CHAPTER 7:
BREAKING THE LAW

Although very few of us realize it, we often hold on to the deep wounds from our childhood and spend the rest of our lives trying to overcome or escape feelings of rejection. Some of us set out to prove to ourselves and others that we are valuable and important by amassing worldly success. Others of us go in the opposite direction and indulge in destructive behaviors. Whether we are billionaires, homeless drug addicts, or somewhere in between, our motivation is the same. We ache to free ourselves from the underlying, nagging feeling that we just aren't good enough.

God uses these feelings of inadequacy to draw us to Him, but the enemy is right there, too. Even after we come to God, the devil wants us to continue feeling like we don't measure up. He twists our perception of the Bible so we overlook or misunderstand what grace really means. He causes us to view the Scriptures through the lenses of the law, or a list of dos-and-don'ts that we think qualifies us for salvation. He attempts to get us to transfer our insecurities into our relationship with God so that we will stay focused on our own shortcomings, missing out on all the glory, power, freedom, and security of walking in true grace.

When we live our Christian lives under the law, we are oppressed and imprisoned. We are held captive by a brutal dictator, called the religious spirit, who demands we make every effort to rid ourselves of sin so that we can be righteous. It sounds noble and right, but it really takes us down the wrong road.

> **Proverbs 14:12** – *There is a way that appears to be right, but in the end it leads to death.*

When we don't look at the Scriptures through the New Covenant lenses of grace, we allow the enemy to put a veil over our eyes so that we go back to an Old Covenant, law-based perspective. Under the law there is a neverending list of sins, shortcomings, weaknesses, character defects, and unhealthy thought patterns that weigh us down and prevent us from ever meeting the standard of personal holiness we think God requires. No matter how much sin we confess, shortcomings we overcome, weaknesses we strengthen, character defects we correct, or unhealthy thought patterns we make right, we will always come up short. There will always be more that we must strive to overcome because it is only by being perfect that we can satisfy the demands of the law.

Without the Holy Spirit taking away the veil so we can see the glory and power of grace, religion will erroneously take the biblical principles that are outlined in the New Testament and use them to define the moral and ethical standards that Christians must live up to in order to be saved. And if others fail at meeting the standards, we will demand repentance or even accuse them of not being true Christians.

If we ever start judging people, we have fallen from grace and are living under the law. We have come under the influence of the religious spirit. The context of the New Covenant is grace, not a standard to live up to, not a new-and-improved version of the law.

Now, should we obey the commands in the Bible? Absolutely! But only in the context of grace, and here's why. If we obey them in the context of law, that is, in order to meet a standard so that we can be accepted by God and by the church, we are rejecting what the cross really accomplished for us. We are saying that what Jesus did wasn't enough—that we must contribute to what it takes to be saved. We are falling from grace and imprisoning ourselves back under a system of performance. It is here, under the law, where sin (a.k.a. Satan) retains power over us.

> **1 Corinthians 15:56** – *...the power of sin [Satan] is the law.*
> (brackets mine)

We are in a power struggle between law and grace, between the spirit of religion and the Spirit of freedom.

> **2 Corinthians 3:17** – *...where the Spirit of the Lord is, there is freedom*

Under law, sin (Satan) has power over us. Under grace, freedom (Jesus) reigns. Under religion, we live by trying to measure up. Under the Spirit, we live in the gift of righteousness. So, who do we want as our master?

> **Romans 6:14** – *For sin [Satan] shall not be your master, because you are not under law, but under grace. (brackets mine)*

Remember, sin is a noun—a person, place, or thing. It is not an action. Under law, Satan is our master. **When we try to live up to a standard to be righteous, we give power to the enemy because every time we fall short, he is right there to condemn us.** When we attempt to meet an expectation in order to be accepted, we invite him to come into our lives but he only comes for one reason.

> **John 10:10** – *"The thief comes **only** to steal and kill and destroy."*
> (emphasis mine)

We give him permission to steal our authority, kill our identity, and destroy our destiny. The name *Satan* means "accuser" and the implication of his name is one of a lawyer accusing a defendant in court. He is an expert in the law—not just the Old Testament law but in law-based thinking, which applies to Christians who use New Testament commands in the same way the Israelites used the Old Testament commands...as a standard for righteousness.

If we allow ourselves to be under the law and we do something that we know is wrong, we will believe that the consequence for this infraction is that we lose some of our righteousness before God. Then the enemy will take full advantage of our incorrect view of grace to launch an assault of judgments against us. He wants us to feel guilty and ashamed of our failure. He wants us to feel like we are not good enough for salvation. He wants us to think that God is disappointed or mad at us. If he can succeed at this, we will lose confidence that God is with us. We will want to hide from God like Adam and Eve did. We will become too consumed with our own shortcomings to walk like Jesus did and radically impact the world.

The enemy will use any failure, weakness, shortcoming, or character flaw we have to get our focus off of Jesus and onto ourselves by accusing us of not measuring up. If we are struggling with a particular sin in our lives, we must ask ourselves, "In what way do I feel like I'm not good enough?" Because that is where the enemy is accusing us, trying to discourage us for not meeting the expectation in some way. It is in these emotions that we turn to sin in an attempt to feel better. We say, "I just need to cut loose a little and have some fun." When we go along with this deception and indulge in sin, we are agreeing with Satan's accusation that we are failures in some way. We give him permission to put us under the law, under the power of sin.

Satan and a host of his demented paralegals will turn up the chatter in our minds every time we mess up and remind us that we are no good, that we are worthless, that if only we had this education, if only we were in better shape, if only we had more money, etc., then we would be wanted, accepted, and loved by God and others.

Feelings of inadequacy and deficiency are based in not meeting someone's standard, whether that standard is from the Bible, our parents, Hollywood, or anywhere else. These feelings can only exist to the extent that we allow ourselves to be under their judgment. **Any area of life where we wish we were better or stronger is the place where the enemy will attempt to condemn us.** Any area where we feel rejection is where he will strike because he was rejected and wants us to experience some of his pain. He is furious at us because he can never be redeemed like we can. He is enraged with bitter jealousy.

Fear not. This very area in which we feel insufficient is where God wants to change our minds. Sometimes He allows the enemy to accuse us in certain ways to expose where we need an upgrade in our thinking about ourselves. That is where we need healing the most. It is where He wants us to agree with His thinking about us and get rid of that out-of-date recording that plays over and over in our minds that we aren't good enough, that we are deficient, that we are worthless. This is where Jesus, the greatest super-hero ever, comes swooping in with grace radiating from His smile and says,

> **Song of Songs 4:7** – *You are altogether beautiful, my darling; there is no flaw in you.*

(Yes, He is even talking to us men. We are, in fact, the bride of Christ, as odd as that may seem in our present reality.)

The overwhelming power of God's unconditional love lifts us right out of the courtroom, where Satan stands accusing us, and seats us with Jesus at the banquet table. Grace takes us to a party being thrown for those who have been acquitted, for those who have had all charges dropped for a lack of evidence. Jesus took away the evidence against us, so now the enemy has nothing to charge us with...ever again.

> **Colossians 2:13-14** – *He forgave us all our sins, **having canceled the written code**, with its regulations, that was against us and*

*that stood opposed to us; **he took it away, nailing it to the cross.*** *(emphasis mine)*

Jesus actually crucified the law. He canceled it, took it away, and nailed it to the cross. Like us, the law was crucified with Jesus. What happened to us when we were crucified with Him? We died and were born again as new creations under grace. The same thing happened to the law. It died and was born again as principles to live by under grace. The law doesn't exist anymore in the same context that it used to. Therefore, there is no basis for accusations against us because there is no law for us to measure up to. There is no more standard to meet because Jesus already did it for us. It's over. *"It is finished."*[10]

Jesus unlocked the power of grace

> **Ephesians 2:15** – ...*by abolishing in his flesh the law with its commandments and regulations.*

The verb *abolish* also means "to destroy," "to do away with," "to render useless or inactive."[11] Jesus destroyed the law, He did away with it, He rendered it useless and inactive by killing it on the cross. It's good news!

> **Romans 10:4** – ...*Christ is the end of the law...*

This might seem confusing in light of what Jesus said in the Sermon on the Mount

> **Matthew 5:17-18** – *"Do not think that I have come to abolish the Law or the Prophets; I have not come to abolish them but to fulfill them. For truly I tell you, until heaven and earth disappear, not the smallest letter, not the least stroke of a pen, will by any means disappear from the Law until everything is accomplished."*

The key here is to remember the context of the Gospels. It is a time of transition but it is still in an Old Covenant context. He is closing out the Old and introducing the New.

One of the challenges with this passage is the word *disappear* which literally means to "pass by" or "pass away."[12] Another point of confusion is the last four words of verse 18, *"until everything is accomplished."* Both of these point us to Jesus' last words that we just quoted above, *"It is finished."* Everything was accomplished at the cross. Everything passed away at the cross. Heaven and earth are now under a new covenant. Because of this change of covenants, the law has been abolished in its old context.

The law being crucified is a big part of the good news and the enemy wants to hide that from us. He wants us under the law because it's his only weapon. He doesn't want us to understand grace because then his influence in our lives is greatly decreased. After we receive the revelation of grace, he can still shoot his arrows of condemnation at us, but they won't have as big of an effect. He can still try to stir up our old hurts of rejection, but the more we feast on grace, the more healing we receive for those old wounds. Soon he won't have anything substantial to throw at us. We will continue to break the power of the law, to increase in our freedom, and to grow in our desire to help others get free as well.

Applying principles, keeping commands, and living up to standards, even if they are biblical, are for secular self-help books if they are not motivated out of an overflowing gratitude for His grace. In fact, when we attempt to do these things to improve our self-worth, we actually put ourselves under a curse.

> **Galatians 3:10-11** – *All who rely on observing the law are under a curse, for it is written: "Cursed is everyone who does not continue to do everything written in the Book of the Law." Clearly no one is justified before God by the law, because, "The righteous will live by faith."*

Attempting to use our performance or obedience as a means to feel good about ourselves curses us with always needing to do more because we will never feel good enough. How we feel about ourselves will be ever changing based on how we perform. If we have a good day, we'll feel good about ourselves, but if we have a bad day, we'll beat ourselves up. With grace, we can always feel good about ourselves because it isn't based on anything we do. Our worth is solely based on His performance, and He performed perfectly on our behalf.

Grace tells us we have immeasurable value and infinite worth. Our value and our worth are determined by the price paid for us. And to our Daddy, we are worth more than the precious blood of Jesus.

Grace communicates God's heart for us, saying, "You are mine because I ransomed you. I ransomed you because I chose you. I chose you because I wanted you. I wanted you because I love you. I love you because you are my son (or daughter)."

Grace invites us to participate in His perfection and it opens us up to everything good that He has for us.

Grace protects us, heals us, makes us whole. Grace satisfies us, accepts us, embraces us. Grace nurtures us, comforts us, encourages us. Grace builds us up, makes us solid, gives us security.

Grace buys us our freedom, and with freedom comes great power. In fact, He gives us

> **Ephesians 1:19-20** – ...*his incomparably great power for us who believe. That power is the same as the mighty strength he exerted when he raised Christ from the dead...*

The same power that raised Jesus from the dead is now ours through grace. The same power that Jesus used to do miracles is now ours through grace. The same power that Jesus used to overcome temptation is now ours through grace. The same power that Jesus had to love the broken and the hurting is now ours through grace.

Grace releases power to repent, to grow, and to be transformed through the Holy Spirit. None of these things happen in the same measure when we simply attempt to apply biblical principles, keep biblical commands, or live up to biblical standards in order to show God we are making every effort to follow Jesus. Only unconditional acceptance changes our mind in a way that is consistent with how He thinks. Only everlasting mercy spurs us to grow so we can be who He made us to be. Only His enduring love compels us to draw closer to Him. **We become more like Him the more we feel safe in the cocoon of His unending embrace.**

Going back to Romans 6:14, who do we want as our master?

> **Romans 6:14** – *For sin [Satan] shall not be your master, because you are not under law, but under grace.* (brackets mine)

When we are under the protective covering of grace, we can be led by the Holy Spirit. Sin cannot lead us when we are under grace. Instead of the law making us feel rejected because we are not good enough, grace makes us feel accepted just the way we are because the burden of the law has been abolished. It has been crucified along with our flesh.

This does not mean that we will never mess up or fall short again. It means that sin can never condemn us again because our covering is grace. In fact, sin itself has been condemned.

> **Romans 8:1-4** – *Therefore, there is now no condemnation for those who are in Christ Jesus, because through Christ Jesus the law of the Spirit [the New Covenant of grace] who gives life has set you free from the law of sin and death [the Old Covenant of expectation]. For what the law was powerless to do [to make us righteous] because it was weakened by the flesh [or sinful nature], God did [made us righteous] by sending his own Son in the likeness of sinful flesh to be a sin offering. And so* **he condemned sin** *in the flesh, in order that the righteous requirement of the law might be fully met in us, who do not live according to the flesh but according to the Spirit.* (brackets and emphasis mine)

Once we enter into the New Covenant, we enter into Christ Jesus where there will never be any condemnation for our sin: past, present, or future. We are now under the law of the Spirit, under the grace of the New Covenant, set free from the law of the Old Covenant where we were constantly accused for our sin. The law was powerless to make us righteous because we inherited a sinful nature from Adam which prevented us from being perfect. But God made us righteous when Jesus offered Himself to be perfect for us, condemning sin instead of condemning us.

If sin has been condemned, there is nothing that can condemn us. The requirement of the law for us to be perfect has been fully met for us by Jesus, and to prove that we are forever perfect in God's eyes, He gave us the Holy Spirit. The Holy Spirit is God, and He cannot dwell in imperfection.

Breaking the power of the law, the power of the religious spirit, and the power of sin is only accomplished by submitting to the undeserved and unearned favor that Jesus purchased for us. Only grace disarms the power of the enemy, makes us perfect, and releases the power of the Holy Spirit to live in us and lead us the rest of our lives. Let us forever rid ourselves of the curse of the law and instead walk in the freedom and power of His unlimited grace.

The next chapter explains how we are free in Christ, but that doesn't mean we can get away with anything we want.

Declarations

- You delivered me from the domain of darkness and transferred me into Your Kingdom of light.

- You are love and there's no fear in love, so I am fearless.

- The power of sin has been broken. I live a victorious life. I am not a victim. I am more than a conqueror.

- I have received You, Jesus, as my Forgiver and my Leader. You have redeemed me from hell and have given me a new destiny.

CHAPTER 8:
FREE BUT NOT LAWLESS

Freedom in the church can be a scary thought for those of us who like things very structured, orderly, and predictable—for those of us who like clearly defined boundaries, established protocols, and pre-set rituals. Freedom in the church can appear to mean that all of these things are thrown out the window and that chaos will ensue. We can fear what could happen if we allow people to worship and encounter God in any way they feel led to. The thought of letting go of our traditions and getting outside of the box, could make us very uncomfortable. Yet, freedom is a cornerstone of the New Covenant.

> **Galatians 5:1** – *It is for freedom that Christ has set us free. Stand firm, then, and do not let yourselves be burdened again by a yoke of slavery [to the law].* (brackets mine)

> **1 Timothy 2:6** – *He gave his life to purchase freedom for everyone...* (NLT)

Many churches struggle with this very issue, which is why Paul addressed it in several letters.

In the Galatian church, the Jewish believers were used to the constraints of the law and to the traditions of their religious culture. So, when Gentile believers were enjoying their freedom in Christ in ways that violated the Jewish traditions, some of the Jews started binding this unfamiliar freedom with what they knew—the law. It was hard for them to let go of control over what the church should look and feel like.

Allowing the Holy Spirit to lead us into new freedom and new experiences requires us to trust that He knows what He's doing. It requires us to give Him permission to be who He really is and to do whatever He wants. But the Jews weren't quite sure what was okay and what wasn't, so they went back to their old ways. As a result, Paul wrote a very pointed letter to the Galatian church, warning them of the dangers of reintroducing the law and mixing it with grace, about combining the religion of the Old Covenant with the freedom of the New, and how it would rob them of the blessings that come from grace alone.

> **Galatians 5:9** – *"A little yeast works through the whole batch of dough."*

In other words, a little law will spread throughout the whole church. Law + Grace = Law. The Old Covenant was a mixture of law and grace, and God called it the ministry of death (**2 Corinthians 3:7**). Religion and freedom cannot co-exist harmoniously. Religion is based in fear; freedom is based in trust. Religion comes from imposing the law on ourselves and others; freedom comes from embracing the grace Jesus purchased. As Pastor Joseph Prince says, "The law demands but grace supplies."[13]

Paul made it abundantly clear to the Galatians that mixing the idea of measuring up to a standard of righteousness together with the idea of trusting

Jesus for salvation was in opposition to the New Covenant of being saved through faith by grace alone.

- Combining law and grace is a perversion of the gospel:

   Galatians 1:7 – *Evidently some people are throwing you into confusion and are trying to pervert the gospel of Christ [with the law].* (brackets mine)

- Coming under the law will stop the Holy Spirit from working miracles:

   Galatians 3:5 – *So again I ask, does God give you his Spirit and work miracles among you by the works of the law, or by your believing what you heard [the message of grace]?* (brackets mine)

- Under the law, we are slaves to the world's ways, despite our efforts to resist them:

   Galatians 4:3, 9 – *So also, when we were underage [under the law], we were in slavery under the elemental spiritual forces of the world... how is it that you are turning back to those weak and miserable forces? Do you wish to be enslaved by them all over again?* (brackets mine)

- Only by the Spirit, not by the law, can we overcome sin:

   Galatians 5:16, 18 – *So I say, walk by the Spirit, and you will not gratify the desires of the flesh...if you are led by the Spirit, you are not under the law.*

The law had its purpose, but that time ended at the cross. Those of us who desire order and clearly defined boundaries because we feel it shows proper respect and reverence toward God, are completely free to relate to Him in this way. At the same time, those of us who enjoy holy laughter, dancing in worship, and the miracle-working power of the Spirit are also free to enjoy

God in these ways. Neither environment is right or wrong. All of it has biblical roots, and we are free to worship God in the way that is comfortable for us. It comes down to a matter of preference, which is why God has different churches take on different forms. Some are quiet and solemn, some are loud and raucous, some are in between. Just because it's different doesn't mean it's wrong. **Anytime we condemn others for being different, we are allowing the religious spirit to lead us into law-based thinking.**

The Bible says that under grace we have the freedom to do anything we want and not be condemned for it. To emphasize this point, God said it four times!

> **1 Corinthians 6:12** – *"Everything is permissible for me"—but not everything is beneficial. "Everything is permissible for me"—but I will not be mastered by anything.*

> **1 Corinthians 10:23** – *"Everything is permissible"—but not everything is beneficial. "Everything is permissible"—but not everything is constructive.*

Paul did not disagree with the Corinthians when they said, *"Everything is permissible for me."* He did, however, issue some warnings that went along with this freedom. Even though under grace we have complete freedom to do anything we want and not lose our salvation, not everything will benefit us or build us up. In fact, some things will enable the enemy to enslave us or master us. This is why we must rely on the Holy Spirit to lead us in how we live as well as how we interpret and apply the Bible.

The Law of the Spirit

When we submit to the Holy Spirit's leadership in our lives, the Bible promises that we *"will not gratify the desires of the flesh."*[14] It is the Holy Spirit's job to guide us, give us direction, and tell us which way to go along with what we need to avoid. Many of us are much more comfortable in following the principles of the Bible than we are in following the Holy Spirit. We put way more time and effort into studying the Bible than we do into developing a relationship with the Holy Spirit.

Now please don't misunderstand. The Bible is hugely important, but it's not more important than the Holy Spirit. Some of us have reconfigured the trinity to be Father, Son, and Holy Bible. If so, we must correct our priorities and invest more into fellowship with the Spirit so that we can have our Bible study bear the fruit He desires.

Unfortunately, the Holy Spirit has been misrepresented in some circles. Some people have done strange and unbiblical things claiming that they were being led by the Spirit. On the other hand, some people have done some horrendous things by taking Scripture out of context. In either case, we cannot allow the excesses of a few misguided souls to rob us of the pinnacle of the Christian life, which is an intimate union with the Holy Spirit.

Just because some of us have had certain experiences that others of us haven't, it doesn't define what is beneficial or even biblical. Some of us have had amazing supernatural encounters with God, and some of us haven't had anything of the sort. Unfortunately, we can tend to use these experiences, or lack thereof, as a means to make doctrines that judge those who have had different experiences. As stated before, just because it's different, it doesn't mean it's wrong.

The Holy Spirit communicated with people in many different ways throughout the Bible. This illustrates that He can choose to interact with us anyway He wants: whether it's through a voice, a dream, a vision, a trance, a knowing, a sign, a miracle, another person, the Bible, etc. There are numerous biblical examples, but God is not contained or constrained by His Book. He is certainly free to do something not written in it. Some of us are so bent on keeping Him in the box of our own understanding or our own experience that we discount or even condemn anything outside of it. When we do this, we like to call it *wisdom* instead of what it really is—fear of what we don't understand.

• When we encounter an expression of the Holy Spirit that goes beyond our understanding, many of us allow the spirit of religion to whip us into a frenzy of fear. We set off on a crusade to protect the church from this perceived threat instead of asking the Holy Spirit to show us if this could be Him expressing Himself in a way previously unknown to us. **When we approach things with preconceived ideas and with doctrines founded on our limited perspective, we can inadvertently reject a powerful blessing that the Holy Spirit is trying to introduce to us.**

Giving into this fear of the unknown over-stimulates our desire to control things. It makes us want to feel safe in what's familiar instead of feeling safe in Daddy's arms and being open to something new that He might have for us.

The power of the enemy to deceive us is not greater than the power of the Holy Spirit to lead us.

It is not our job to use the law to control and police how the Holy Spirit works. The Holy Spirit has His own laws to police us, so we need to trust that He can handle His job.

> **Romans 8:2** – ...*through Christ Jesus* **the law of the Spirit** *who gives life has set you free from the law of sin and death.* *(emphasis mine)*

The law of the Spirit is grace. Grace gives life and sets us free. The law of sin and death is the Old Covenant law. The law of sin and death refers to dead works where we vainly try to attain or maintain our own righteousness by meeting a standard. What it really does is cause us to be enslaved by sin and kills our souls (which is why it's called the law of sin and death). Through grace (the law of the Spirit), the Holy Spirit sets us free from sin's rule and, in its place, crowns righteousness as our new master.

Romans 6:18 – *You have been set free from sin and have become slaves to righteousness.*

Now that sin is no longer our master, the Spirit has replaced it with righteousness in Christ.

Under the law, we focus on judging the sinfulness of ourselves and others. Under grace, we focus on how the gift of righteousness has set us free to live in the glorious state of God's never-ending acceptance. Instead of striving for approval through our obedience, His gift of righteousness frees us to do what is good without the threat of rejection.

Through the law of the Spirit, righteousness has become our master. Now the Holy Spirit does not convict us of our sinfulness; rather, He calls us to live up to the righteousness that is now over us. He says to us, "What are you doing living like this when you are a son of the King? Get out of this mess and go home to Daddy. Start living like the prince you are, and expand the King's domain through the power and authority of your sonship."

In the New Covenant, we are new creations with a heavenly DNA, completely righteous and holy in Christ. Being convicted of sin is Old Covenant. Now when we mess up, we are convicted of not living out our true identity as a royal priest, a warrior bride, and a beloved son or daughter. (More on this in Chapter 9)

This might seem like semantics but it's bigger than that; it's Old Covenant verses New. The old perspective says we are not good enough—that we fail to measure up. The new says that we are better than how we are living—that we are already victorious. One tears us down and the other builds us up. One focuses on the negative and the other on the positive. One attempts to motivate us to change through shame by bringing us lower, while the other attempts to motivate us to change through inspiration by calling us higher.

Even though the law of the Spirit is freedom, it does not ignore sinful behavior. It empowers us to live above it, where as religion condemns us to repeat it. Condemnation will never produce the level of change that freedom will because condemnation is based in fear. Freedom is based in love, and love is infinitely more powerful to transform us than fear is.

Law in a New Context

Although we are now under the freedom of the law of the Spirit, it doesn't mean we can do anything we want without consequence. **Freedom in Christ is not a license to sin. It merely refers to the fact that we are free from trying to measure up to a standard in order to be righteous with God.** We are free from ever having to worry about our salvation. We are saved and righteous because of what Jesus did for us and not because of anything we do or don't do.

Sin is never okay; it does not please God and it is not what He wants for us. In addition to the law of the Spirit there are other laws by which we must live because

> **1 John 3:4** – ...*sin is lawlessness.*

Even though we have been set free in Jesus, there are still laws that apply to our lives. Doing something the Bible says is wrong or that goes against our conscience violates these laws. It impedes our freedom. Freedom is not lawlessness where we take advantage of grace. Freedom is unconditional acceptance. Now that we are out from under the law of the Old Covenant, we are completely accepted just the way we are by trusting in what Jesus did. To keep us living in freedom in the way He intended, God gave us other laws that the Bible speaks of in a variety of ways.

> **Romans 3:27-28** – *Where, then, is boasting? It is excluded. Because of what law? The law that requires works? No, because of **the law that requires faith**. For we maintain that a person is justified by faith apart from the works of the law.*

> **Romans 7:21-23** – *So I find **this law** at work: Although I want to do good, evil is right there with me. For in my inner being I delight in **God's law**; but I see **another law** at work in me, waging war*

*against **the law of my mind** and making me a prisoner of **the law of sin** at work within me.*

Romans 8:7 – *The mind governed by the flesh is hostile to God; it does not submit to **God's law**, nor can it do so.*

Galatians 6:2 – *Carry each other's burdens, and in this way you will fulfill **the law of Christ.***

(emphasis mine)

As American citizens, we are free, but there are still many kinds of laws we must live by. If we break them, there are corresponding consequences. However, no matter what laws we break, we can never lose our citizenship. It's the same for heaven.

Philippians 3:20 – *...our citizenship is in heaven.*

Being born again means we were born into a permanent citizenship in heaven. There are laws we must live by if we are to enjoy the benefits of our citizenship. We must also obey these laws to avoid the consequences that come from breaking them. We know these laws because we have the Holy Spirit living inside us and because we have the Bible to spell things out for us. When we cross the border from the domain of darkness into His Kingdom of Light, He gives us an amazing promise concerning these laws of freedom.

Jeremiah 31:33 – *I will put my laws in their minds and write them on their hearts.*

Hebrews 8:10 – *I will put my laws in their minds and write them on their hearts.*

Hebrews 10:16 – *I will put my laws in their minds and write them on their hearts.*

He repeats this three times because He wants us to trust that He will walk each one of us through our own journey. Our journeys can look very different from one another. When we try to get each other to conform to what we think the journey is supposed to look like, we limit the freedom He purchased and we are actually attempting to play God's role in that person's life. Everyone has different backgrounds, experiences, ways of thinking, wounds to be healed, etc., and the spirit of religion wants to force us into a one-size-fits-all way of thinking.

Religion says that if someone doesn't fit in with our way of thinking, they are sinning against God and we must condemn them in order to defend God's honor. Religion will manipulate the meaning and application of freedom by using Scripture out of context to condemn it. It will make us think we are serving God by taking a stand.

Religion is threatened by freedom but grace is not. Grace isn't even threatened if we use our freedom to sin. It's way too vast and powerful to be threatened by something that's already been condemned and defeated.

God's laws are multi-faceted and multi-dimensional. There are many ways to look at and apply them. The Bible says that even the law of the Old Covenant, that Jesus set us free from, still applies to our lives.

> **Romans 7:12** – *So then, the law is holy, and the commandment is holy, righteous and good.*

> **1 Timothy 1:8** – *...the law is good if one uses it properly.*

Hey, wait a minute! How can the law be good if it brings sin and death? Context is everything. **Under grace, we use the principles of the law to live our lives in a way that brings honor to God.**

For example, we should apply to our hearts that anger is like murder and that lust is like adultery. We should love our enemies and not just our neighbors.

We should bless those who persecute us. We should never lie and always rejoice with the truth. We should honor our parents.

The laws are good in and of themselves, but under grace we are free from ever being condemned when we fall short in putting them into practice.

We must make every effort to live in a way that is consistent with the laws of God. The more we do so, the more He will be able to use us to fulfill His purposes in our lives and in the lives of those we influence.

Something Old, Something New

When we become Christians, one of the things that keeps us from continuing to rebel against God's laws is the fact that our old sinful nature was crucified with Jesus, and in its place we received a new nature, a divine nature. The sinful nature tends to view life from an Old Covenant context of trying to measure up. That's why the enemy wants us under the law. It gives power to the sinful nature to keep us enslaved to sin. Our new divine nature, however, views life from a New Covenant context of being accepted just as we are. It knows that we are royalty, that we are already victorious, and that we are blameless in Christ.

> **Galatians 5:24** – *Those who belong to Christ Jesus have crucified the flesh [sinful nature] with its passions and desires. (brackets mine)*

> **2 Peter 1:4** – *...he has given us his very great and precious promises, so that through them **you may participate in the divine nature** (emphasis mine)*

Not only was our sinful nature crucified with Jesus, it was also cut away from our heart in a spiritual circumcision.

> **Romans 2:29** – *...[This] circumcision is circumcision of the heart, by the Spirit, not by the written code...*

Colossians 2:11 – *In him you were also circumcised with a circumcision not performed by human hands. Your whole self ruled by the flesh [sinful nature] was put off when you were circumcised by Christ... (brackets mine)*

Even though our sinful nature was crucified with Jesus and was circumcised out of our hearts by the Spirit, it still exists and can have influence in our lives. How is this possible? Although we were crucified and raised with Christ, we are still here in these human, pre-resurrection bodies. The law was also crucified with Christ, yet it is still being used by the enemy to accuse us and keep us enslaved to sin. All pain and sickness was crucified with Jesus, yet both can still afflict us, even those of us who know how to walk in authority over such things. **Just because something was accomplished in the spirit realm, doesn't mean it automatically manifests in the physical.** This is one of those paradoxes that we can't fully understand on this side of eternity.

Although the Bible teaches that we have a crucified and circumcised sinful nature, we must still choose to not allow it to lead us in our freedom because this is also what the Bible teaches:

Galatians 5:13 – *You, my brothers, were called to be free. But do not use your freedom to indulge the sinful nature; rather, serve one another in love.*

Galatians 5:16-17 – *So I say, live by the Spirit, and you will not gratify the desires of the sinful nature. For the sinful nature desires what is contrary to the Spirit, and the Spirit what is contrary to the sinful nature. They are in conflict with each other, so that you do not do what you want.*

Colossians 3:5 – *Put to death, therefore, whatever belongs to your earthly nature: sexual immorality, impurity, lust, evil desires and greed, which is idolatry.*

Ephesians 4:22-24 – *You were taught, with regard to your former way of life, to put off your old self [sinful nature], which is being corrupted by its deceitful desires; to be made new in the attitude of your minds; and to put on the new self [divine nature],* **created to be like God in true righteousness and holiness.** *(brackets and emphasis mine)*

In one verse, the Bible instructs us not to indulge our sinful nature. In another, it informs us that our sinful nature has desires that are contrary to the Spirit and that it is in conflict with the Spirit. Other verses tell us to put our sinful nature to death (even though it's already been crucified) and to put it off (or cast it away).

All of these verses speak of the sinful nature as something that we still have to deal with; even though the Bible also says it's dead and has been cut away from our hearts. It's both; like Jesus is 100 percent God and 100 percent man.

In the freedom we now have, we must be intentional about protecting ourselves against our sinful nature. If we are to fulfill God's desires for our lives, we must choose to live by the Spirit and to guard our hearts against allowing the sinful nature to influence us.

As new creations with a divine nature, we are now predisposed to do what is right and pleasing in His sight (i.e. slaves of righteousness). The sinful nature used to be at the core of who we were. Through our death, burial, and resurrection with Jesus, we now have a new divine nature at our core. Our resurrection with Jesus not only endows us with a divine nature, but also qualifies us to have the Holy Spirit take up residence in us. **This combination of having a divine nature and the Holy Spirit inside of us empowers us to use our freedom in accordance with God's laws.** We can live above our old sinful nature, which is no longer in a position of leadership.

Our new selves have been *"created to be like God in true righteousness and holiness"* (Ephesians 4:24), and we are not only well-equipped to obey God, but also to lead and inspire the world through the freedom and power we have. Because we are completely free to be who He made us to be, as well as to live our lives without any fear of ever being condemned, we can be the calm in the storm that the Holy Spirit can use to draw the lost toward salvation. By staying focused on His goodness, we can maintain our peace and joy through trials, speak the truth in love, not judge others, and not indulge in the things of the world.

> **Galatians 5:19-21** – *When you follow the desires of your sinful nature, the results are very clear: sexual immorality, impurity, lustful pleasures, idolatry, sorcery, hostility, quarreling, jealousy, outbursts of anger, selfish ambition, dissension, division, envy, drunkenness, wild parties, and other sins like these. Let me tell you again, as I have before, that anyone living that sort of life will not inherit the Kingdom of God.* (NLT)

This passage is one of many that seems to indicate that if we follow the desires of our sinful nature we will lose our salvation. In light of everything we have looked at so far, it should be clear that grace means that it is impossible to lose our salvation. So the question is, what does *"inherit the Kingdom of God"* refer to?

Bullinger's lexicon describes it as the following: "the kingdom of God, the sphere of God's rule, as being then present among the Jews in the person of Christ (Luke 11:20; 17:21, marginal). Then, the sphere of Christ's workings; now the sphere of the Holy Ghost's workings (Romans 14:17. 1 Corinthians 4:20)."[15]

In the Bible, we witness the Kingdom of God in the ministry of Jesus when He walked the earth. Now we see it displayed through the work of the Holy Spirit. When the Bible mentions inheriting or not inheriting the Kingdom of God based on how we live, it is not referring to heaven because we are already eternally seated with Jesus in heaven.

Paul is saying that after we become Christians and we live a life dominated by sin, we will not experience the workings of the Holy Spirit. We will not walk in the Spirit's power and authority or benefit from the fruits of the Spirit. We will not have *"peace that transcends understanding"*[16] and *"inexpressible joy.*[17] We will put ourselves back under the law, under the rule of sin, allowing Satan to be our master.

When we use our freedom to indulge in sin, we break God's laws and miss out on how He wants His Kingdom to be manifested through us.

If we are not living by the Spirit, the fruits of the Spirit will shrivel up.

> **Galatians 5:22-23** – *But the Holy Spirit produces this kind of fruit in our lives: love, joy, peace, patience, kindness, goodness, faithfulness, gentleness, and self-control.* (NLT)

If we are living contrary to the Bible, to the Holy Spirit's leadership, and to God's laws for us, we will produce the opposite of these fruits, which will inspire no one to find out more about Jesus. Who would want to follow someone who was apathetic, grumpy, anxious, impatient, mean, evil, unfaithful, insensitive, and self-indulgent? How we live matters a great deal in how we experience the Holy Spirit and in how we are able to attract the lost toward the One who gives life.

We possess what every person needs, so it is of utmost importance that we obey the Scriptures and follow the lead of the Spirit. **If we are to bring Him glory, we must follow the laws we read in the Bible and the laws He writes on our hearts and minds.** The more we live up to the life He calls us to, the more He can use us to win the world.

The Law of Grace

The New Testament is full of instructions, commands, and laws regarding what we should do and what we should not do, how we should think, how we should feel, etc. It spells out what is good and what is evil. It tells us how to have healthy relationships, what to do in certain situations, how to handle money, how to resolve conflicts, how to raise children, etc. The list goes on and on.

Religion will tell us that if we don't obey these things, we will lose our salvation, or we were never saved to begin with. Religion makes Christianity about how well we obey commands, follow instructions, and adhere to laws. It also glosses over what the cross did for us, or it has us only focus on how Jesus took the punishment for our sins, so we will live in a constant state of shame and guilt over it. It makes Christianity about us instead of about what He did. Religion says if we disobey to a certain degree, we forfeit what Jesus did for us, or if we indulge in certain sins for a certain amount of time or stop going to church. then we become lost again.

Grace is the cornerstone of Christianity. It is the immovable truth of the New Covenant. It is the foundation that everything is built on. Grace is the cross. The cross is grace. Jesus is grace. Grace is undeserved favor. Grace is unmerited. **Grace cannot be received or held on to through obedience because that violates the very definition of grace.**

Was Abraham called righteous when he obeyed God and left his home? No. He was called righteous when he believed that God would do for him what he could not do for himself (i.e. give him a son in his old age). We are Abraham's children if we believe and not if we obey.

Grace is not given as a result of following instructions because then it would be merited. It would be earned. Grace has no line we can cross to lose our salvation because then we would deserve it by measuring up to not crossing that line. If grace is undeserved in the first place, how could we do something to deserve it being taken away? That goes against the definition of grace.

Grace is the highest law. It is the law of love, the law of the Spirit, the law of Christ. Grace is God's unbreakable law that was written in His blood. The shed blood of Jesus is the most powerful means by which any covenant could ever be made, and He chose to make the New Covenant of grace with it.

Because His blood is eternal, the covenant we entered when we believed is eternal. It can never be broken by anything done in time. We cannot allow the enemy to use this evil spirit of religion to blind the eyes of our heart to this fact.

The laws, instructions, and commands we have in the New Testament are for our benefit not for our condemnation. They are designed to protect us and to bring us closer to Him. The main reason they are there is so we can know Him better. They are provided so we can experience Him more. When we choose to ignore them, we miss that opportunity to grow closer to Him. Since we don't live in a vacuum, the people in our lives are affected both when we obey the Scriptures and also when we don't.

Let us read the Scriptures with grace lenses so that grace remains clear and focused in our hearts and minds. And let us do our best to obey them. **If there are passages that seem to be inconsistent with grace, we can ask the Holy Spirit to reveal their meaning to us. We can't throw out the very definition of grace so we can force wrong interpretations of these difficult Scriptures to fit into our paradigm.** We must be still and wait on the Lord. We must maintain that He is good and He is faithful. His mercies are everlasting. He will open up the right understanding at the right time. Again, it is always better to have unanswered questions than to have the wrong answers.

Grace means freedom, but we must also obey Him if we are to walk in our true identity. In Chapter 9: Rags to Riches, we will see how we go from spiritual poverty to eternal royalty and explore our true identity in Jesus.

Declarations

- I am free from needing to measure up to any standard in order to receive or keep my salvation.

- I can worship in whatever way I feel You are leading me.

- I don't have to judge those with different experiences.

- I choose to live by Your laws, so I can draw closer to You and receive all that You have for me.

- I give You permission to do whatever You want in my life.

CHAPTER 9:
RAGS TO RICHES

Most of us love a great story of someone who started out struggling in poverty, barely scraping by, and how they mustered up the will to work hard, be disciplined, stay positive, and end up becoming hugely successful. We like to see someone on the bottom come out on top. It gives us hope. It inspires us to want to overcome any obstacles we have in our own lives.

This is not one of those stories. This is God's story. Yes, we play a part in it, but only a small one. He does all the work and we are the beneficiaries. He does the rescuing, and we let Him rescue us.

Before that can happen, we must realize we need to be rescued—that we need someone to save us. Without this revelation, what Jesus has done for us is of no consequence. The cross makes no difference to us unless we see ourselves as lost. In fact, the Bible says we will think it's foolishness.

Getting to the point where we find ourselves in a place of great spiritual need is a journey in and of itself. This is what the Holy Spirit is working on while we are wandering around out there in the world. We must get to a place of frustration and hopelessness, where we are desperate for answers because nothing seems to satisfy the ache in our souls.

Jesus tells a famous story about one such man: The Lost (or Prodigal) Son.

> **Luke 15:11-24** – *Jesus continued: "There was a man who had two sons. The younger one said to his father, 'Father, give me my share of the estate.' So he divided his property between them.*
>
> *"Not long after that, the younger son got together all he had, set off for a distant country and there squandered his wealth in wild living. After he had spent everything, there was a severe famine in that whole country, and he began to be in need. So he went and hired himself out to a citizen of that country, who sent him to his fields to feed pigs. He longed to fill his stomach with the pods that the pigs were eating, but no one gave him anything.*
>
> *"When he came to his senses, he said, 'How many of my father's hired servants have food to spare, and here I am starving to death! I will set out and go back to my father and say to him: Father, I have sinned against heaven and against you. I am no longer worthy to be called your son; make me like one of your hired servants.' So he got up and went to his father.*
>
> *"But while he was still a long way off, his father saw him and was filled with compassion for him; he ran to his son, threw his arms around him and kissed him.*
>
> *"The son said to him, 'Father, I have sinned against heaven and against you. I am no longer worthy to be called your son.'*
>
> *"But the father said to his servants, 'Quick! Bring the best robe and put it on him. Put a ring on his finger and sandals on his feet.*

Bring the fattened calf and kill it. Let's have a feast and celebrate. For this son of mine was dead and is alive again; he was lost and is found.' So they began to celebrate.

Most of us can relate to this story in one way or another.

The first thing that happened to the son after his partying had run its course was that *"he began to be in need."* He finally started to feel the void in his life, his hunger for significance and meaning. It was always there, but he allowed himself to believe the lie that it could be satisfied in the shallow and fleshly things of this world. Sometimes it takes waking up in a situation that we never thought we would find ourselves in, one of embarrassment, shame, and compromise, before we acknowledge the hole in our heart that was there all along.

For the son, the physical hunger illustrated the emptiness in his soul. The job of feeding pigs illustrated his lost identity. The distance from home illustrated how far he had wandered away in his heart. When his neediness finally outweighed his desire to do things his own way, Jesus was finally able to get through to him, and *"he came to his senses."* At last he decided to let Jesus pick him up and take him home, back to his father's house.

> **Isaiah 53:6** – *We all, like sheep, have gone astray, each of us has turned to our own way...*

Like the lost son and the lost sheep (which we discussed in Chapter 4), all of us have wandered away from God and have eventually found ourselves in a needy position, a lost state, or a hopeless situation. We were spiritually bankrupt, living in rags, so to speak, broken and alone. We had hit bottom.

In fact, we were worse than at the bottom. We were below bottom. Not only were we lost, we also owed a huge debt we could never pay, as Jesus shares in this story.

> **Matthew 18:23-27** – *"Therefore, the kingdom of heaven is like a king who wanted to settle accounts with his servants. As he*

began the settlement, a man who owed him ten thousand bags of gold was brought to him. Since he was not able to pay, the master ordered that he and his wife and his children and all that he had be sold to repay the debt.

"At this the servant fell on his knees before him. 'Be patient with me,' he begged, 'and I will pay back everything.' The servant's master took pity on him, canceled the debt and let him go."

The passage above actually says the amount the servant owed was 10,000 talents. A talent was an amount of money worth twenty years of a servant's wages. If we translated that into today's dollars at only $10 per hour it comes to $4 billion!

The servant in the story represents us and the king represents God. Jesus is illustrating that the debt we owe God for our sinfulness is way more than we could ever possibly repay.

The forgiveness of our sin is really a debt being paid for us that we could never afford to pay ourselves. Our sins aren't forgiven because we confess them, feel bad about them, and commit to never do them again. Our forgiveness is more like a bank transaction or a business deal between the Father and Jesus.

When the Bible talks about our sins being forgiven, it actually doesn't come across in our culture like it would in the original languages. A better translation would be that our sins were canceled, in the same way as having a debt forgiven. What we owed God, or could ever possibly owe Him due to any sin, has been completely wiped out. In the heavenly ledger, our huge debt has been stamped "paid in full."

1 Peter 1:18-19 – *For you know that it was not with perishable things such as silver or gold that you were redeemed from the empty way of life handed down to you from your ancestors, but with the precious blood of Christ, a lamb without blemish or defect.*

So imagine that Jesus walked into the Bank of God and paid our bill for us. Because He paid it with His blood, that is, with something infinitely more valuable than money, not only was our debt canceled, but our account was credited with more than we could ever spend! We went from being hopelessly over our heads in debt to being the richest people on the planet! Now that's good news!

Later on in the story of the Prodigal Son, the dad reminds the older brother who stayed home

> **Luke 15:31** – *"My son,"* the father said, *"you are always with me, and **everything I have is yours.**"* (emphasis mine)

Our Father, the God of the universe, has made us His sons and daughters and, as a result, has promised us everything He has. We get it all. The entire Kingdom is ours right now!

Notice that the father didn't tell the son that everything he has **will be** his but that it **is** his. Present tense. When we are transferred from the kingdom of darkness to the kingdom of light, from lost to saved, from orphans to beloved children, He opens the storehouse and immediately gives us everything.

Pastor Brent Lokker reiterates in his amazing book *Always Loved,* something he has said for years, **"To the degree that you believe who you already are in Christ, you will walk in what you already have."**[18] It's important for us to slow down and chew on this statement because it has huge implications and can shift our whole paradigm to be more in line with God's. Read it several times so it sinks in. The more you know who you are, that is, who God says you are, the more you can tap into the infinite resources of His eternal kingdom. This idea might prompt us to ask something like, "Who am I in God's eyes?" and "What does salvation get me besides going to heaven in the end?"

Who Are You?

This is not an easy question for most of us to answer because we typically don't take the time to stop and force ourselves to assign words to it. We may give it some fleeting thought, but not serious contemplation or definition. Yet the more we really dig in and are intentional about believing and knowing who we are in Christ, the more we will live our lives in the power and the riches that are available to us. **Knowing our identity in Him (i.e. who He says we are) is the most important key to becoming more like Him.** The more we become like Him, the more we can walk as He did by tapping into what's already at our disposal.

The enemy knows this, so he strikes at this issue repeatedly in our lives. If he can keep us in the dark about our heavenly identity, he can limit our impact on the world and our effectiveness in destroying his works. He did it with Jesus several times, trying to get Him to doubt who He was in order to detour Him from His pre-ordained destination.

> **Matthew 4:3** – *The tempter came to him and said, "If you are the Son of God, tell these stones to become bread."*

He will continually attack us by whispering lies in our minds and by using other people to get us to doubt who God says we are. "You call yourself a Christian but look at how easily you give in to sin. A real follower of Jesus wouldn't do such things." "If people knew the real you, they would see you for the fraud you are." "Is God going to answer the prayers of someone so pathetic?"

The enemy will even use Scriptures to attack us. One of his favorites is

> **Romans 12:3** – *Do not think of yourself more highly than you ought, but rather think of yourself with sober judgment...*

He will twist this verse to try and make us think we could never do anything great or world-changing by getting us to focus on ourselves. And if we do, he is right.

The point of this verse isn't to lower our opinion of ourselves but to shift our attention to who He says we are in Christ and to know that by trusting Him we can do anything, literally. The rest of this passage reveals its context and

and its real meaning. It talks about how we all have gifts from the Holy Spirit and that we shouldn't think that our gifts are better than someone else's.

Our identity in Christ must be clear if we are to follow the path God wants us to walk. If we listen to the enemy's whispers to make us doubt who Daddy says we are, we will miss living in the abundance of everything that is already ours.

Sons and Daughters

> **Galatians 4:6-7** – *Because you are sons, God sent the Spirit of his Son into our hearts, the Spirit who calls out, "Abba, Father." So you are no longer a slave, but a son; and since you are a son, God has made you also an heir.*

We already looked at a similar Scripture in Romans and how *Abba* means "Daddy" or "Da da." It is the most familiar and intimate term for *father* that there is in Hebrew. If we were to go to Israel today, we would still hear the little children calling out to their daddies, "Abba, Abba," as they hold their arms up so their papas can pick them up and carry them. That is how our Daddy longs for us to relate to Him.

It is the Spirit of Jesus in us that calls out, "Abba." The more we allow the Holy Spirit to lead us, the more comfortable we become with viewing our Heavenly Father as our tender and gentle Daddy. Although many of us have daddy issues that will require significant inner healing, we must do our best not to frame our Heavenly Father in the same light as our physical fathers.

Intimacy with God breeds security, security breeds trust, and trust breeds peace. When we experience His continual peace in our hearts, we won't fear anything. We will walk in the reality of His unshakeable and eternal kingdom, not swayed by circumstance. We will live from a place that is above the worries and cares of this world. Whatever happens, even if it is painful at the time, we will know for certain that He will eventually somehow work it out for good.

John 14:27 – (Jesus speaking) *"Peace I leave with you; my peace I give you. I do not give to you as the world gives. Do not let your hearts be troubled and do not be afraid."*

The peace of Jesus is a product of His closeness with Daddy and is a gift to us. He is inviting us to have a similar father-child relationship with God the Father that He had, living every moment of life in His peace; untroubled and unafraid.

The meaning of this word for peace carries with it many connotations. It is more than just a feeling of tranquility, although it does include that. It also means the end of striving or strife. That is, we do not have to fight anymore for victory in any part of life because the fight is over, the victory is already won. This peace means being in a state of health or well-being emotionally, mentally, physically, spiritually, relationally, financially, etc. It's a trouble-free zone for every area of life. No matter what chaos is taking place all around us, we get to choose to let the Holy Spirit take us to Daddy, where we can raise our arms and say, "Up, Daddy." We can choose to not let our hearts be troubled or afraid because being a son or daughter sitting on Daddy's lap is the secret to contentment.

Philippians 4:11-13 – *...for I have learned to be content whatever the circumstances. I know what it is to be in need, and I know what it is to have plenty. I have learned the secret of being content in any and every situation, whether well fed or hungry, whether living in plenty or in want. I can do all this through him who gives me strength.*

This peace is beyond our understanding **(Philippians 4:6-7),** and it is available to us simply because we are sons and daughters of the most kind-hearted, gracious, and nurturing Father ever. He already knows exactly how every detail of our lives will play out, so we can live in His secret place of rest—the place that the whole world is longing for. Everyone wants this peace, this security, this contentment. Those who are ripe for it will be able to sense it or see it in us, especially when we cruise unstressed through situations that most people would be freaking out over.

Our status as beloved sons and daughters can usher us into His presence every minute of every day. We simply have to choose to be aware of it. Being His children also qualifies us for a glorious inheritance. We are heirs with Jesus!

Heirs and Heiresses

Many of us want a rich family member to leave us an inheritance. We watch movies and television shows with a twinge of envy when some lawyer is reading a will and dividing up a huge fortune amongst the heirs. Well, we don't have to envy anymore because we are now heirs as well. Not heirs to just some worldly fortune—heirs of **everything**.

We have seen this word *heir* mentioned a few times, but it's worth going into a little deeper because it has some pretty large implications.

> **Romans 8:17** – *Now if we are children, then we are heirs—heirs of God and co-heirs with Christ…*

> **Galatians 3:29** – *If you belong to Christ, then you are Abraham's seed, and heirs according to the promise.*

We are co-heirs with Christ and heirs according to the promise that God gave Abraham. A co-heir means that we all share the entire estate together, as opposed to the estate being divided amongst us separately.

An heir according to the promise means that it is unchangeable. God made a promise to Abraham and God cannot lie, so He cannot break the promise. In Christ, we are included in that promise to Abraham because Christ is the rightful heir of Abraham.

Being a co-heir with Christ says that whatever belongs to Jesus is now ours as well. So what belongs to Jesus?

> **Matthew 28:18** – *Then Jesus came to them and said, "All authority in heaven and on earth has been given to me."*

It's all His. Jesus is in charge of everything. All the riches and resources of this world are at His disposal. Every power and blessing of heaven are available to Him. The entire Kingdom of God, which encompasses everything that was created as well as that which is eternal, belongs to Jesus; therefore, it all belongs to us. Right now!

He has brought us from the pit of being overwhelmed with a massive debt we could never repay to the pinnacle of being the most wealthy, blessed people who ever lived. It's good news!

The first and most important part of our inheritance is the Holy Spirit.

> **Ephesians 1:13-14** – *Having believed, you were marked in him with a seal, the promised Holy Spirit, who is a deposit guaranteeing our inheritance until the redemption of those who are God's possession—to the praise of his glory.*

The Holy Spirit is a down payment of what is to come. He is a *"deposit **guaranteeing** our inheritance."* The Holy Spirit has been sealed up inside of us, so we will know without a doubt that our salvation is a done deal.

This verse clearly says that our inheritance is guaranteed! He could not live in us if we were not perfectly spotless and totally free from the stain of sin. **The blood of Jesus has permanently and completely washed us clean, so that we can inherit God.**

Along with our salvation being irrevocable and with God now permanently residing inside us, Scriptures inform us that everything is ours.

> **Romans 8:32** – *He who did not spare his own Son, but gave him up for us all—how will he not also, along with him, graciously give us **all things**?*

> **Colossians 3:21-22** – ***All things are yours**, whether Paul or Apollos or Peter or the world or life or death or the present or the future—all are yours...*

> (emphasis mine)

Although this is an amazing thought, it is a little vague. It's hard for us to wrap our minds around it. Let's try to get a little more specific so we can have confidence in our time of need. We need to understand more clearly who we are and what is ours, so we can walk out our lives with the security of beloved sons and daughters, heirs and heiresses.

> **2 Corinthians 8:9** – *For you know the grace of our Lord Jesus Christ, that though he was rich, yet for your sakes* **he became poor, so that you** *through his poverty* **might become rich.**

> **Ephesians 1:18** – *...the riches of his glorious inheritance...*

> **Ephesians 3:8** – *...he graciously gave me the privilege of telling the Gentiles about* **the endless treasures available to them in Christ.**

> **Colossians 1:27** – *...the riches and glory of Christ are for you...*(NLT)

> (emphasis mine)

There are many other verses that speak of the riches and the glory that are included in our inheritance. Many of us gloss over the fact that they all speak of financial wealth. That is what the Greek word translated *riches* means. It doesn't mean spiritual riches, emotional riches, relational riches, etc. It's true that we are rich in these ways, too, but these passages do not express those things. These verses are specifically talking about financial abundance.

Many of us want to guard ourselves from the sin of greed to the point where we think it's godly to be poor. How can we be a blessing to the world when we are poor? Is Jesus poor? If it is more blessed to give than to receive, we should be eager to give a lot. To give a lot, we must have a lot.

Because our inheritance includes financial prosperity, He will give it to us in the amount that we can faithfully steward. If He cannot trust us to manage it well and to use it how He intends, we must mature in this area. Jesus became poor so that we could be rich.

- Although financial blessing is available to us as part of our inheritance, we certainly have the freedom to refuse it, but is that really what His will is for us? If not, we must prepare ourselves to handle wealth by putting biblical financial principles into practice. **The lessons we learn in handling worldly riches prepare us for being good stewards of more important things.**

> **Luke 16:11** – (Jesus speaking) *So if you have not been trustworthy in handling worldly wealth, who will trust you with true riches?*

The implication here is that God will use how we manage our money to determine whether or not we can successfully manage the more valuable things of the Kingdom. We must learn to control our spending, pay off any financial debt, save for emergencies, and invest to build wealth. Then we will be able to take care of our families as well as contribute to the needs of others and fund the expansion of the Kingdom. If we can prove trustworthy in this little thing, He can trust us with more.

Financial riches are not available to us so that we can live lavish lifestyles and indulge in worldly pleasures. That would be following the path of the Prodigal Son. Riches are a testing ground, a school of Kingdom training. How we handle money, and the freedom it affords, reveals our hearts.

Financial success is also a prophetic sign to the world of the spiritual riches we have in Christ. When misguided, yet spiritually hungry, people see how we handle our wealth using biblical principles—living modestly and giving generously—they will be intrigued by our motivation to do such things. Our lifestyle will command respect as well as open doors to deeper conversations about the Kingdom of God.

Financial wealth is a good example of a worldly resource available to us through our inheritance but what spiritual resources are included in our inheritance?

Ephesians 1:3 – *Praise be to the God and Father of our Lord Jesus Christ, who has blessed us in the heavenly realms with **every spiritual blessing** in Christ.* (emphasis mine)

In Jesus, we are blessed with every spiritual blessing. What does that mean? Obviously, our sin debt has been canceled. That alone is an enormous spiritual blessing that is beyond words. But as we said before, He didn't just wipe out our debt. He also filled our account.

Romans 4:4-8 – *Now when a man works, his wages are not credited to him as a gift, but as an obligation. However, to the man who does not work but trusts God who justifies the wicked, his **faith is credited as righteousness**. David says the same thing when he speaks of the blessedness of the man to whom **God credits righteousness apart from works**: "Blessed are they whose transgressions are forgiven, whose sins are covered. Blessed is the man whose sin the Lord will **never** count against him."* (emphasis mine)

The biggest spiritual blessing we inherit is that God credits our account with the righteousness of Jesus: His very own righteousness. And He does so without us having to work for it. We receive God's righteousness as a gift, as part of our inheritance, not by measuring up to a standard of obedience. If we had to live up to a certain expectation, it would be a wage or an obligation and not a gift. An inheritance is not something we are owed as a result of meeting some criteria.

Notice that the passage says that God *"justifies the wicked,"* and not the righteous, because we trust Him to do so *"apart from works."* We inherit eternal righteousness because we trust in what Jesus did for us. Period.

Another spiritual blessing that we inherit is power in our soul and spirit.

Ephesians 3:16 – *I pray that **from his glorious, unlimited resources he will empower you** with inner strength through his Spirit.* (emphasis mine)

Our souls are considered to be our mind, will, and emotions. Our spirits are where the Holy Spirit resides and where we connect with God. This is our "inner man." Out of the wealth of His glory, He empowers us by His Spirit to align our will with His. He gives us the strength to be unified with His purposes and, in that, to be courageous and content.

This inner strength is what enables us to overcome the struggles and troubles of the world and to walk in confidence that He can and will deliver us at the right time and in the way He chooses. Things won't typically work out in the way we imagine or hope they would. If they did, it wouldn't require faith. Faith is being sure of what we do not see even in our imagination or our spiritual sight.

There are many more spiritual blessings we could explore, but eternal righteousness and inner power are just a few examples to whet our appetite.

So we are sons and daughters of the King as well as heirs and heiresses of His Kingdom. Put these together and they add up to us being royalty.

Kings and Queens

Many of us are fascinated with royalty. It seems so regal and romantic, suave and sophisticated. We can be in awe of the wealth, power, and privilege that come from being in a royal family. Even from young ages, little girls love to play princess, as if they instinctively know that they were made to be royalty.

Indeed we are! We are sons and daughters of the King. We were reborn into the royal family and, as new creations, we now have royal blood coursing through our veins. As such, we were made to rule.

> **Romans 5:17** – *For if, by the trespass of the one man, death reigned through that one man, how much more will those who receive God's abundant provision of grace and of the gift of righteousness* **reign in life** *through the one man, Jesus Christ!* (emphasis mine)

The Greek word translated *reign* carries with it the connotations "to be king, to possess regal authority, to rule, to have kingship."[19] Through Adam, death used to be king and rule over us. Now through the grace and righteousness we received from God in Christ, we *"reign in life."* We are now kings and queens. We now possess regal authority.

Jesus is called the King of kings not only because He reigns over the kingdoms of this world, but also because He is our King. It is a reference to everyone in His kingdom. We are the kings that He is King over.

Royalty means we are men and women of honor, of class, of integrity. The Bible's instructions and commands reveal how we are to live as royal ambassadors of the kingdom. They teach us that we should be generous, gracious, kind, loving, honest, etc. **Every command in Scripture that applies to us is there for us to express our royal identity, to mold our character as a royal representative, and to extend the bounds of the royal kingdom.**

In order for us to do this, He seated us with Him on the throne.

> **Ephesians 1:20-21** – *...he raised Christ from the dead and seated him at his right hand in the heavenly realms, far above all rule and authority, power and dominion, and every name that is invoked, not only in the present age but also in the one to come.*

> **Ephesians 2:6** – *And God raised us up with Christ and seated us with him in the heavenly realms in Christ Jesus...*

Because we are seated with Jesus, far above every created thing, we carry with us the highest authority, an eternal authority established outside of time. We are not like the kings and queens of this world, temporarily ruling an earthly kingdom. **We rule over life itself because we sit on the throne with the Author of Life, with the One who created life.** Supreme confidence and boldness should be ours that we would be given such a seat of honor and authority.

With such kingly authority, every word we say has power. Words create reality and we can use them to build up or tear down, to bring life or to bring death, to bless or to curse. As kings, our words carry great weight, so we must make every effort to speak the very words that God would speak. Again, this comes from intimacy with Him, knowing His heart of kindness and compassion, and revealing it in what we say.

As kings and queens, what we do reverberates throughout the kingdom. Every action or inaction makes a difference and alters reality in some way, both in the natural realm and in the spirit realm. If we think what we do doesn't matter, we are being deceived. We do not exist in a vacuum. Our actions directly and indirectly impact people and atmospheres either positively or negatively.

> **Ephesians 5:15-16** – *Be very careful, then, how you live—not as unwise but as wise, making the most of every opportunity, because the days are evil.*

When we are *"very careful,"* living as *"wise"* royals, we will be able to make the most of the opportunities we have to advance the King's will. We will expand the King's domain, tapping into the vast resources at our disposal. He has made available to us everything we need for every good work which He has prepared for us. And in all that we do, we represent the King and His Kingdom, so it is of utmost importance that we represent Him well.

Many of us have spent most of our lives thinking and feeling, to some extent, like we were a nobody, an outcast, a loser. We believed that we were worthless and didn't make much of a difference. For us to make the paradigm shift to thinking and feeling like kings and queens requires a complete transformation of our self-image. This is no easy task and typically does not happen overnight. It takes us being intentional about transforming our minds through meditating on what He has done for us. It happens by looking into His Word, allowing Him to highlight truths that build up our royal identity, and then chewing on those truths until we get a deeper revelation of who we are. The purpose of revelation is to draw us closer to Him. The closer we are to Him, the more we know who we are and understand our value. **Our worth to God is reflected in the price He paid for us.**

In a nutshell, the kingly anointing is meant for extending the King's domain, advancing the Kingdom, and taking territory away from the enemy. It is marching forth in power and authority, attacking and overthrowing the works of the enemy, and releasing the kingdom of God to invade people's lives and the places we walk. (More on this in Chapter 10.)

Priests and Priestesses

It is a stretch for many of us to grasp being a king or queen, but our stretching is not over. We also have another amazing identity in His glorious riches for us: that of being priests and priestesses. The Bible says that we

> **Isaiah 61:6** – ...*will be called priests of the Lord, you will be named ministers of our God.*

> **1 Peter 2:5** – ...*are being built into a spiritual house [or a temple of the Spirit], to be a holy priesthood, offering spiritual sacrifices acceptable to God through Jesus Christ.*

> **1 Peter 2:9** – ...*are a chosen people, a royal priesthood, a holy nation, God's special possession, that you may declare the praises of him who called you out of darkness into his wonderful light.*

(brackets mine)

We have a great and eternal High Priest in Jesus who ministers to the Father from a place of rest, seated next to Him. We, being seated with Jesus, are all priests along with Him and we also minister to God.

Peter calls us holy in both passages. *Holy* means being "different from the world, that is, being like God; set apart for God, to be, as it were, exclusively his."[20] He has separated us out from the world and we are now His *"special possession."* Because He ransomed us from our captor, purchased us out of slavery, and redeemed us from our debt, we belong to Him and are in His employ.

In addition to holy, Peter also calls us royal. The word for *royal* also means "kingly or a body of kings,"[21] reinforcing our identity as kings and queens.

Kings and priests in the Old Testament were anointed with oil as a sign of their position and authority. Our anointing for these roles is with the oil of heaven, that is, the Holy Spirit, qualifying us as **eternal** kings and priests. Jesus is both a King and a Priest. Because we have His oil, His Spirit, we have the same anointing.

We already touched on what it means to be a king, so what does it mean for us to be priests?

As Peter points out in the verse above, we were made into a royal priesthood so that we, *"may declare the praises of him who called* [us] *out of darkness into his wonderful light."* Part of a priest's role is to offer sacrifices on behalf of and for the benefit of others. Because Jesus offered the final blood sacrifice, the primary way we minister to the Lord as New Covenant priests is by offering a sacrifice of praise.

> **Hebrews 13:15-16** – *Through Jesus, therefore, let us continually offer to God a sacrifice of praise—the fruit of lips that openly profess his name. And do not forget to do good and to share with others, for with such sacrifices God is pleased.*

We can offer a sacrifice of praise in many ways. We can sing His praises, we can shout them, we can speak them to ourselves, we can speak them to others, we can pray them, we can paint them, we can dance them, etc. The ways to praise Him are unlimited. Anything and everything we do could be a sacrifice of praise if we do it with that intent. The Holy Spirit can inspire our creativity to take us to greater depths of His love by revealing different ways to praise and worship Him.

Our praise lets us enjoy more of His presence. It also fills us up with more of Him. This filling is for more than the warm, fuzzy feelings we get from it, although those feelings are really cool. Priests offer sacrifices for the benefit of others, so our praises to Him are to fill us to the point where we overflow, blessing those we contact or pray for.

As verse 16 points out, we also minister to others by remembering to do good and to share what we have been blessed with. Good deeds and sharing are part of our priestly duty; obviously, our motive for doing them is not because it's our duty but because we are compelled by the love we have received.

Part of this sharing with others includes telling people the gospel.

> **Romans 15:15-16** – *...because of the grace God gave me 16 to be a minister of Christ Jesus to the Gentiles.* **He gave me the priestly duty of proclaiming the gospel of God...** *(emphasis mine)*

Some of the functions of being kings and priests overlap, but the priestly anointing is mainly where we get filled up to walk out the kingly anointing. Through praise and worship as priests, we rest in His glory and goodness. Through prayer and intercession, we shift atmospheres and change tides. By soaking in His presence, we are saturated with His love and mercy. All of these are designed for Him to flow through us with rivers of living water that, as kings, we use to bring life to the dead, hope to the hopeless, and comfort to the hurting.

Our identity and our inheritance are critical for us to be who He created us to be and to do the things He has prepared for us to do. In the next chapter, we will look at what we are supposed to do with this royal identity and glorious inheritance.

Declarations

- You give me abundant provision to meet every need for me, my family, and those I minister to.

- I am a co-heir with Jesus. Everything in heaven and on earth is my inheritance right now.

- I am a child of the King. I have been adopted into the royal family with full rights and privileges.

- I am a king in Christ. I walk in power, authority, and confidence.

- I am a priest in Christ. I worship, praise, and serve my God wholeheartedly.

Chapter 10:
Walk This Way

Growing in the different aspects of what grace means, who we are in Christ, and what we have available to us is great, but how do we effectively translate it into action? What do we do with it? How do we "walk it out"?

As Christians, we not only trust in Jesus as our Savior, but we also submit to His lordship. He is our Master, Teacher, and Leader. A disciple is someone who imitates their master in every way. We are to think as He did, believe as He did, love as He did, and act as He did. Our mission in life is to become as much like Jesus as possible; to re-present Him to the world so people may come to know Him better. His purpose and His methods must be our purpose and methods.

Jesus revealed His purpose in the following verse.

> **Luke 19:10** – *For the Son of Man came to seek and to save the lost.*

And His methods are summarized nicely in this passage

> **Acts 10:38** – *...God anointed Jesus of Nazareth with the Holy Spirit and power, and...he went around doing good and healing all who were under the power of the devil, because God was with him.*

Jesus was anointed with the Holy Spirit and power. This enabled Him to do good and heal those under the power of the devil. We see Him freeing people from demonic oppression, healing the sick, raising the dead back to life, feeding the hungry, offering compassion to the hurting, extending grace to the sinful, confronting the religious, and teaching about the Kingdom.

Jesus' intimate relationship with the Father and the Holy Spirit produced a ministry of extraordinary results. Whether He did something miraculous or spoke grace-filled words, He transformed people's lives. Just one touch or one word from Jesus was the most profound spiritual experience anyone ever had. His power and authority were awe inspiring. His grace and compassion were heart melting. His kindness and generosity were overwhelming. In short, Jesus was amazing.

How are we supposed to follow such a man? How are we to do what He did? How can we have an impact anywhere close to what Jesus had?

The main purpose of receiving grace from God is to extend grace to others. Jesus gave grace to people in a lot of different ways. Most of us are comfortable extending grace in things like feeding the hungry or offering compassion to the hurting, but we have a hard time believing that we could also show grace to people by healing the sick and raising the dead. And that's okay. If we haven't felt the Spirit prompt us to pray for God's supernatural power to do the miraculous, we need to follow where the Holy Spirit is leading.

However, many of us get excited in our spirits to see God do supernatural works through us. Perhaps we just need a little more faith and some practical instruction in order to take the risk. If that's the case, seek out ministries that are "doing the stuff" as they like to say. There are tons of them all over the world who regularly pray for and experience miraculous signs like blind eyes and deaf ears opening, cancers disappearing, limbs being restored, financial provision at just the right time, etc.

Grace unlocks the power of the cross to walk in victory over the things of this world. He defeated everything that the enemy uses to steal, kill, and destroy. It is our right as royal ambassadors of His Kingdom to trample on anything of the devil, including sickness, poverty, hopelessness, worthlessness, fear... even death.

Whether we confirm the message of God's love and grace with miraculous signs or not, the important thing is for us to listen closely to the Holy Spirit and follow the path He has for us. At the very least, He wants us to model grace by accepting everyone wherever they are on their journey and offering them the same kind of unconditional love that He offers us.

A Ministry of Miracles

Many of us love to read about Jesus and the disciples performing miraculous signs. We try to imagine what it would be like to see a shriveled hand restored right before our eyes or a paralytic get up and start dancing around. In John 12:25, the Bible says that Jesus did so many miracles through the Holy Spirit that if we were to write them down, the earth couldn't hold all the books! By far the most common miracle the Holy Spirit did through Jesus was to heal people physically.

Jesus put aside the powers of His Godhood and related to the Father completely as a man to show us what an intimate relationship with the Father and the Holy Spirit can be like when we are righteous in God's sight. Jesus was righteous before the Father because of His perfect obedience. He was intimate with the Father because of His prayer life. We, however, are righteous because Jesus was perfectly obedient on our behalf. Our righteousness in God's sight grants us the same access to intimacy with the Father and the Holy Spirit that Jesus had.

Jesus was compelled by love and empowered by the Spirit to destroy the devil's work with demonstrations of His amazing grace. Many times He extended grace by performing supernatural wonders to prove He really was the Son of God. During His ministry, He trained His followers to imitate Him in this way as well. Nothing has changed. If we would like to demonstrate God's grace with miraculous signs as the Spirit prompts us, the door is open.

> **John 14:12** – *(Jesus speaking)* *"Very truly I tell you,* **whoever believes in me will do the works I have been doing,** *and they will do even greater things than these, because I am going to the Father."* (emphasis added)

Jesus clearly expects those who believe in Him to do the same works of grace He did. These works include preaching the good news, caring for the poor, comforting the hurting, healing the sick, driving demons away from people, and raising the dead.

To illustrate that a Spirit-led ministry of signs and wonders was available to everyone who followed Him, Jesus commanded the disciples to go out and do it. They received hands-on training in how to release the Kingdom of God into the lives of the hurting and the lost.

> **Matthew 10:1, 8** – *Jesus called his twelve disciples together and gave them authority to cast out evil spirits and to heal every kind of disease and illness..." Heal the sick, raise the dead, cure those with leprosy, and cast out demons. Give as freely as you have received!"*

> **Mark 6:12-13** – *So the disciples went out, telling everyone they met to repent of their sins and turn to God. And they cast out many demons and healed many sick people, anointing them with olive oil.*

> **Luke 9:1-2, 6** – *One day Jesus called together his twelve disciples and gave them power and authority to cast out all demons and to heal all diseases. Then he sent them out to tell*

everyone about the Kingdom of God and to heal the sick...So they began their circuit of the villages, preaching the Good News and healing the sick.

He started with His twelve disciples and, once they were experienced, He opened the training up to seventy-two other disciples.

> **Luke 10:1, 9, 17** – *The Lord now chose seventy-two other disciples and sent them ahead in pairs to all the towns and places he planned to visit... "Heal the sick, and tell them, 'The Kingdom of God is near you now.'"... When the seventy-two disciples returned, they joyfully reported to him, "Lord, even the demons obey us when we use your name!"*

Not only did regular rank-and-file followers of Jesus command sickness to be healed, demons to flee, and the dead to be raised while Jesus was alive, they continued to do so after He ascended to heaven and they were baptized with the Holy Spirit.

On a practical note, when Jesus sent the disciples out, He told them to *"heal the sick"* not to "pray for the sick." We are to command sickness to leave, the body to be healed, and the demons to flee in the name of Jesus. This is the way Jesus did it and the way the disciples did it. We are to exercise our authority in Christ through the power of the Holy Spirit over everything that is from the devil in the same way that Jesus and His followers did.

As we discussed earlier, one of the Holy Spirit's main roles on earth is to get everyone saved. What better way to do so than to have the sick or hurting experience healing in their bodies? Or have the oppressed experience freedom from demonic influence? Typically we are impacted much more by supernatural encounters with God than we ever could be by church fellowship, Bible stories, and principles for holy living. A supernatural touch from God communicates that He has compassion for our needs. In performing miracles for us, God reveals His heart of grace.

The first century Christians not only shared the message of Jesus and demonstrated love to people, they also confirmed their message with miraculous signs.

Acts 3:4-7, 12; 4:9-10 – *Peter and John looked at [the lame man] intently, and Peter said, "Look at us!" The lame man looked at them eagerly, expecting some money. But Peter said, "I don't have any silver or gold for you. But I'll give you what I have. In the name of Jesus Christ the Nazarene, get up and walk!"...Then Peter took the lame man by the right hand and helped him up. And as he did, the man's feet and ankles were instantly healed and strengthened...Peter saw his opportunity and addressed the crowd..."Do you want to know how [the lame man] was healed? Let me clearly state to all of you and to all the people of Israel that he was healed by the powerful name of Jesus Christ the Nazarene..."* (brackets mine)

Acts 4:29-30 – *"And now, O Lord...Stretch out your hand with healing power; may miraculous signs and wonders be done through the name of your holy servant Jesus."*

Acts 5:12, 14-16 – *The apostles were performing many miraculous signs and wonders among the people...more and more people believed and were brought to the Lord—crowds of both men and women. As a result of the apostles' work, sick people were brought out into the streets on beds and mats so that Peter's shadow might fall across some of them as he went by. Crowds came from the villages around Jerusalem, bringing their sick and those possessed by evil spirits, and they were all healed.*

Acts 6:8 – *Stephen, a man full of God's grace and power, performed amazing miracles and signs among the people.*

Acts 8:4-8 – *But the believers who were scattered preached the Good News about Jesus wherever they went. Philip, for example, went to the city of Samaria and told the people there about the Messiah. Crowds listened intently to Philip because they were eager to hear his message and see the miraculous signs he did. Many evil spirits were cast out, screaming as they left their victims. And many who had been paralyzed or lame were healed. So there was great joy in that city.*

The Bible is awesome and full of incredible stories, but nothing compares with a personal encounter with the All-Mighty One.

This type of ministry kicks open the door of our hearts to want a relationship with such a kind-hearted and powerful God. When we are healed or freed, we can't deny what just happened. It instantly ignites our faith. It creates a desire to want more of Him.

The impact of miracles, signs, and wonders is not just on the ones who were healed or set free. It also transforms those who witness or hear about such events. That's why Jesus' ministry methodology is so necessary in our world. We long for experience—especially supernatural experience. We don't just want to hear principles or stories; we want to encounter the power and presence of the Creator. This spiritual hunger for the unseen realm is one reason many people get turned off by church and end up turning to the occult.

When we combine supernatural experiences with grace-filled fellowship and the power of the Word, it creates a driving passion for more of Him that can't be duplicated in any other way.

Jesus commands us to

Matthew 28:19-20 – *"...go and make disciples of all nations... teaching them to obey everything I have commanded you. And surely I am with you always, to the very end of the age."*

Making disciples of Jesus means that we re-create Him in the lives of those who say yes to His salvation. Our goal is to imitate Him in everything He taught and everything He did. Since Jesus promises to be with us we can safely assume that He desires to minister through us in the same way that He did when He physically walked the earth. We can love unconditionally as He did. We can give grace abundantly as He did. We can minister supernaturally as He did.

If we are uncomfortable with the supernatural part because we don't understand it or it just seems weird, it's okay. Our relationship with Him is unique. We all have our own path to walk and our own different gifts. But let us be open to a supernatural lifestyle and a ministry of the miraculous if that is the direction He wants us to go. We can pray something like, "Holy Spirit lead me in everything I do, just like You did with Jesus. Show me how You want me to follow in Jesus' footsteps. If I am to minister with miraculous signs, please open that door to me and make it obvious. I want You to use me in any way You desire. In Jesus' name, amen."

If we already have the desire to walk in signs and wonders, God will bring it about in the right time. The anointing and boldness to minister like Jesus is born out of our relationship with the Holy Spirit, out of our desire to be more like Him, and out of us knowing who He says we are. The more we encounter and experience God's supernatural presence, power, love, tenderness, etc., the more He transforms us to be like Jesus. Jesus said we will have rivers of living water flow from us. They will rush forth to those longing for a sign from God, those desperate for a miracle, a touch from the Eternal One.

> **1 Corinthians 12:4-11; 27-31** – *There are different kinds of gifts, but the same Spirit distributes them. There are different kinds of service, but the same Lord. There are different kinds of working, but in all of them and in everyone it is the same God at work.*
>
> *Now to each one the manifestation of the Spirit is given for the common good. To one there is given through the Spirit a message of wisdom, to another a message of knowledge by means of the*

*same Spirit, to another faith by the same Spirit, to another gifts
of healing by that one Spirit, to another miraculous powers, to
another prophecy, to another distinguishing between spirits, to
another speaking in different kinds of tongues, and to still another
the interpretation of tongues. All these are the work of one and
the same Spirit, and he distributes them to each one, just as
he determines.*

*Now you are the body of Christ, and each one of you is a part of
it. And God has placed in the church first of all apostles, second
prophets, third teachers, then miracles, then gifts of healing, of
helping, of guidance, and of different kinds of tongues. Are all
apostles? Are all prophets? Are all teachers? Do all work miracles?
Do all have gifts of healing? Do all speak in tongues? Do all
interpret? Now eagerly desire the greater gifts.*

Not everyone has the same gifts. Not everyone works miracles or heals the
sick. The Holy Spirit distributes the gifts as He determines. Just because we
don't have one of the gifts now doesn't mean He won't give it to us as some
point. *"He distributes them to each one"* of us in the measure we can properly
steward. We all have gifts now and we all have more gifts available to us as we
grow. Let us find out how to use them in accordance with the Spirit and let us
"eagerly desire the greater gifts."

It is also important to understand that God values all the gifts and not just the
one(s) we have or are familiar with. We are to show honor to everyone who is
walking in their gifts and also to those who have yet to embrace theirs.

Miracles through Time

Some of us believe that because we now have the Bible, we don't need the
miracles, signs, and wonders anymore. Nowhere in Scripture does it even
hint at the idea that at some point we will need to break away from the model
that Jesus gave us. It doesn't say that we will one day need to replace His

ministry methods with merely attempting to apply biblical principles to our lives. The Bible not only gives us principles, it gives us samples of what God wants to do through us supernaturally in order to save the world.

"It's hard to have the same fruit as the early church when we value a book they didn't have above the Holy Spirit they did have."[22] Bill Johnson

Too much of the church has withdrawn from ministering in supernatural power because of unbelief. We simply don't believe that we can perform miraculous signs through the Holy Spirit like Jesus did. But Jesus did not change His ministry style; He established it, practiced it, and taught it. He doesn't change. His early followers continued in His footsteps as did great men and women of faith throughout the centuries following.

In his thorough, straight-forward, and fascinating book, *2000 Years of Charismatic Christianity*, Eddie L. Hyatt documents how the Holy Spirit continued to do miraculous signs through the lives of those who pursued intimacy with the Holy Spirit. Here are a few examples.

Irenaeus (A.D. 125-200)

"Some truly and certainly cast out devils. The result is that those who have been cleansed from evil spirits frequently both believe and join themselves to the church. Others have foreknowledge of things to come. They see visions, and they utter prophetic expressions. Still others heal the sick by laying their hands upon them, and the sick are made whole. What is more, as I have said, even the dead have been raised up and remained among us for many years."[23]

Hilarion (A.D. 305-385)

Jerome, (A.D. 347-420) who produced what became the official Bible of the Catholic Church, the Latin Vulgate, witnessed Hilarion calm a raging sea that was about to destroy a village. A wall of water caused by an earthquake was heading for

Epidaurus and when Hilarion raised his hands, the sea became completely calm. Jerome goes on to say, "Time would fail me if I wished to relate all the miracles which were wrought by him."[24]

Gregory the Great (A.D. 540-604)

Gregory became Pope in 590 and "recorded many miracles of which he had personal knowledge, including raising the dead."[25]

Martin Luther (1483-1546)

Luther, who began the Reformation, is quoted as saying, "Often has it happened, and still does, that devils have been driven out in the name of Christ; also by calling on His name and prayer, the sick have been healed."[26]

There are many more examples throughout history and up to the present day. Notable people like Tertullian (A.D. 160-240), Augustine (A.D. 354-430), Francis of Assisi (1181-1226), and John Wesley (1703-1791) performed or wrote about miraculous signs done in the name of Jesus.

Ministries Today

Many Christians today are seeing the Holy Spirit perform signs and wonders similar to those we read about in the Bible and throughout history. These are not people who have whacky theology and live on the edge of society, unrelateable to the mainstream of Christiandom. These are people who love the Word, are rooted in sound doctrine and have very intimate walks with the Lord. They are "normal" everyday folk who also happen to believe that God is still in the miracle business and business is booming. Here are some samples.

Iris Ministries

One ministry where we are seeing some amazing miracles is with Roland and Heidi Baker in Mozambique, Africa. In their book, *Always Enough: God's*

Miraculous Provision Among the Poorest Children on Earth,[27] they share how they spent many years in Mozambique working very hard to convert people and build churches but had little fruit to show for it. All of their preaching, teaching, and loving did not impact people's hearts in the way they were hoping and yet they knew that this was the mission field that God had called them to.

Confused and discouraged, they took a trip to Toronto because they had heard that God was pouring out His Spirit at the Toronto Airport Christian Fellowship in an unusual way. While there, Heidi was overcome by the Holy Spirit such that she was not able to move for days. During that time, she had amazing encounters with Jesus, and He promised to give her the entire country of Mozambique. Upon returning to their mission field, the Bakers had incredible favor establishing orphanages and saw God touch these lost children. Miracles and healings started happening in their midst, completely transforming these children from thieves to evangelists.

The Bakers were led to set up their stage in a nearby village. Heidi had a strong sense from the Holy Spirit about someone getting healed of deafness. The crowd gathered and she asked if there was anyone in the village who was deaf. There was. The deaf person went up on the stage and Jesus restored hearing in front of everyone. The entire village was instantly converted! This began their new ministry model (one like Jesus), and in just a few short years they established **thousands** of churches plus several orphanages and ministry schools which regularly experience miracles, signs, and wonders through the power of the Holy Spirit.

Bethel Church

In the small city of Redding, California, there is a church that is making a worldwide impact with all that God is doing there. Bill Johnson, Senior Pastor of Bethel Church, had prayed for many years about revival and seeing people healed and delivered but had yet to witness any results. Although they followed Jesus' model by regularly laying hands on the sick, the injured, and the diseased, nothing happened. Refusing to give up they continued visiting other places where healings were happening. The gates were finally opened and miraculous healings broke out. They now see daily miracles but not just in the church. They also go out on the streets or to the mall to pray for people to be healed. It has become common knowledge around the city that if anyone needs a miracle they should go to the mall and find the Christians from Bethel Church.

This church now has a school of supernatural ministry with thousands of Christians attending from all over the world—those who are hungry to take Bethel's healing anointing and culture of honor back to their home churches and to the mission field. Similar schools are popping up around the world, training Christians how to walk in the love, grace, power, and authority that Jesus modeled and that is available to us through intimacy with Daddy, Brother, and Spirit. (See *Finger of God* by Wanderlust Productions.)

Doug Addison

In addition to healing and deliverance, another way that Jesus ministered was by giving people words of knowledge or encouragement that touched their hearts and drew them to God. Some Christians are finding creative ways to do this same thing. Doug Addison enjoys speaking life into people using dream, tattoo, and piercing interpretation. We have a generation of young people who are more pierced and tattooed than ever before. Doug sees this as people advertising their life experiences and destinies. Most of them are eager to talk about their tattoos or piercings and receive a spiritual interpretation of them. He trains people how to do this and has seen many people healed, delivered, and converted as a result.

Festivals

Some Christians set up stations at New Age festivals or street fairs in different cities without using any religious terms. The goal is to draw in those who are spiritually hungry but may not currently be interested in Christianity. Once there, life-giving words from the Creator's heart are spoken specifically to them. Many of these people powerfully experience God's presence and His touch for the first time. They get a taste of the real thing, and once they have the best, nothing else will satisfy. God is using things like this to plant seeds in people and to grow their desire for Him. Some have also been healed, delivered, and converted on the spot.

Door-to-door

Another growing trend in bringing the love of God to those in need is to simply knock on their door. This sounds pretty intimidating to most of us but there are Christians who are doing this with amazing results. Don Pirozok (www.donpirozok.com) travels around the country and takes teams of local believers out to canvas neighborhoods. In three and a half years they have led over 4,000 people to the Lord. How is this happening? One reason is it's biblical.

> **Acts 5:42** – *Day after day, in the temple courts and **from house to house**, they never stopped teaching and proclaiming the good news that Jesus is the Messiah.* (emphasis mine)

Another reason is because they offer to pray a blessing over the household. It's surprising how disarming this is. It goes something like this, "We are from different churches in the area and have been praying for our city. Now we are going door-to-door to pray personal blessings over families. Is there someone sick we can pray for? Do you need a financial breakthrough? Peace in your marriage? Surely there's something you would like to see going better." Eventually the resident agrees to get prayer. In general, everyone enjoys receiving a blessing. Many times those who need healing are healed. Other times the Presence of God shows up is tangibly felt by all. At that point introducing them to Jesus becomes much easier. They can't help but want to know more about what they just experienced.

These new believers are not just left on their own to flounder in their faith. Everyone who comes to Christ gets follow up visits for fellowship and Bible studies, eventually getting plugged into a local family of believers to be mentored.

Personal Experience

A Day at the Beach

One summer, my family and some friends drove up the coast of Northern California and spent the 4th of July in a town called Crescent City, a little south of the Oregon border. It was a beautiful afternoon at the beach with temperatures in the low 70s and very little wind. But, as is typical on this part of the coast, the fog started coming in. There was a massive fog bank moving up from the south and, having lived at the beach in San Francisco, I knew our gorgeous day was swiftly coming to an end. The temperature would drop about twenty degrees and the cold, wet wind would make playing in the sand and surf unbearable. We had only been at the beach for about thirty minutes, and I didn't want the kids' fun to end so quickly.

I decided to take a leap of faith and claim authority over the weather like Jesus did when He calmed the wind and the waves. I commanded the fog bank stop, for the sun to burn it away, and for the wind to die down, among other things. I prayed like this for about ten minutes while our kids and their friends were playing in the waves. But the fog bank just kept coming up the beach. I was starting to get discouraged and to doubt that this was going to work. Just then, all the kids came back to dry off and have a snack. After a little while, they went back out to play. Having been distracted by the kids, I forgot about the fog bank, so I turned to see where it was. To my amazement, it hadn't just stopped coming up the beach, it had actually retreated! It literally turned around and went the other direction, completely staying away from our part of the beach so the kids were able to enjoy their day in the sun until they were ready to go. I was in awe!

Barroom Boogie

One Saturday night, my wife and I were enjoying a beer at a local alehouse. I had just come from a street fair where we were speaking encouraging words from the Holy Spirit into people's lives. We were also doing some tattoo interpretations at the fair. Our female bartender had some tattoos, so we asked if she would like us to interpret the spiritual meaning of them. She seemed a little hesitant but finally agreed after we assured her it wouldn't be anything bad. When we told her what we felt the Holy Spirit was putting on our hearts, her face lit up. She was so excited that God not only knew about her challenges and struggles but that He was proud of her and how she had overcome them.

A woman sitting next to us who was a Christian in a more conservative denomination couldn't help but hear everything we said to the bartender. She was very intrigued by it. We started chatting and really hit it off. After telling us about herself, she asked us how we came to the point of being able to listen to the Holy Spirit and minister to people. We told her about our many years as Christians living under the law and then how God introduced us to the Holy Spirit and grace. We also told her how God confirmed our decision to seek more of the Holy Spirit when I was led to lay hands on my son and command that he be healed of celiac disease—which he was. Her eyes grew really big as she said, "I have celiac disease."

A lot of people have never heard of this disease, so the chances of running into someone who actually has it are quite slim. Her case was more severe than our son's. If she even had a small dose of gluten (a protein from grains), she would be sick for a week with symptoms similar to the stomach flu. We asked her if she would like us to pray for her to be healed and she readily agreed. Afterwards, my wife gave the woman her phone number so that she could tell us if she was healed. We didn't hear anything, so we assumed that she hadn't been healed. A month after praying for the woman, my wife got a text. Because the woman had such an intense reaction to gluten, she was reluctant to test if she was healed or not. Finally, like our son, she tried a nibble of a Ritz cracker and waited. No reaction. A few days later, she tried again. No reaction. She gradually increased the test amounts and never had any symptoms. It took her so long to text my wife because she wanted to be sure she was healed. Thank you, Jesus!

My wife jokingly says, "We have the bar ministry."

The Most Excellent Way

Gifts and miracles are pointless without sharing the love and grace that God showers upon us.

> **1 Corinthians 13:1-3** – *If I speak in the tongues of men or of angels, but do not have love, I am only a resounding gong or a clanging cymbal. If I have the gift of prophecy and can fathom all mysteries and all knowledge, and if I have a faith that can move mountains, but do not have love, I am nothing. If I give all I possess to the poor and give over my body to hardship that I may boast, but do not have love, I gain nothing.*

We can see incredible signs and wonders in the name of Jesus, but if we do so without His love flowing through us, we will not bear the fruit God desires. Expressing His love is the most important thing. Communicating God's total grace to people reveals His true heart for us. **Signs and wonders are to confirm the message of God's grace.** Although the message is more important than miraculous signs, God often uses the supernatural to grab the attention of those who are open to Him but at the same time are not interested in the message by itself.

How we express God's love is up to our relationship with Him and how the Holy Spirit leads us. Whether we are helping the poor or raising the dead, our ministry must always demonstrate God's grace.

> **Galatians 5:6** – *The only thing that counts is faith expressing itself through love.*

Next up is Part III, which contains new ways to look at many Scriptures that seem to contradict what grace is.

Declarations

- I release the Kingdom of God on earth.

- Jesus, You have given me authority over sin, sickness, death, the works of the devil, the flesh, demons, and the world. I receive my authority and I exercise it.

- In You, I have overcome the world. I am 100% emotionally, physically, spiritually, and mentally healed and whole. I release divine healing to others.

- I am the light of the world, and I displace darkness.

- I declare that every plan or action of the enemy intended to harm me or my family be turned into an amazing blessing in the name of Jesus of Nazareth.

PART III

LOST AND FOUND
IN TRANSLATION

BACKGROUND

After years of searching for truth and for answers to the pointlessness that life seemed to hold, I became a Christian my last semester in college. However, it was in a church that many mainstream Christians considered a cult. We gained that label because we felt like anyone who was not part of our family of churches was most likely not a true Christian.

What made our church unique was that we went on a quest to restore the standards of what we thought the Bible taught a Christian was and how we should live. We were motivated to do this because we saw many people who claimed to be Christians but didn't live according to what the Bible taught in terms of purity, honor, integrity, openness, fruitfulness, and humility. We were tired of the hypocrisy of lukewarm "church-ianity" and wanted a group of sold-out disciples of Jesus who would go anywhere, do anything, and give up everything to evangelize the world. If someone was not willing to live up to that standard, then, according to our view of the Bible, they weren't real Christians.

The paradigm we lived in was simple: spend time with God, study the Word, see where we were falling short, repent, and obey. Introspection was the primary means to spiritual growth. We needed to find something that we didn't feel good about, some area where we weren't measuring up so we could overcome it with God's help through prayer, Bible study, and talking about it. It's an effective model to a certain degree, but the burden of always striving to meet an unattainable expectation eventually wore us down to the point where we couldn't take it anymore. It's no wonder so many people came and went through our doors.

(Please understand, it is not my intent to dishonor my prior church of eighteen years. They are very sincere in their faith and work harder than most at attempting to honor God with their lives. They truly desire to be close to Him and to help others do the same. I pray they experience ever-increasing revelations of God's unfailing love and the full extent of grace that Jesus purchased for us with His blood.)

During my last five or so years in that church, I hit a spiritual ceiling. I felt I had gone as high as I could go in my walk with God. Since I didn't want to be one of those people who became "hardened by sin's deceitfulness" (Hebrews 3:13), I stuck around, doing my best to live a "righteous" life, but longing for more. I knew there had to be something else. I started praying, "God, if there is more than this, I want it. I want to be led by the Spirit like it says in Romans 8. I want to live in the joy of salvation and the peace that is beyond understanding instead of wondering if I'm still saved because I fell short in some way. If there is more to this Christian life, then I need You to show me." I prayed this off and on for a few years before God opened the door.

Through various circumstances, I got in touch with a friend of mine who had "fallen away" from our church a few years earlier. He shared some experiences he regularly had with the spiritual realm. He talked of interactions with angels, demons, and the Holy Spirit and how his life now looked like something right out of the Gospels. He described how, through the Holy Spirit, he was driving out demons, healing the sick, prophesying, seeing miracles, etc. I had no reason to doubt him and it sounded a lot more biblical and exciting than the Christianity I was experiencing. I wanted in on it.

Shortly after visiting with him and getting introduced to the supernatural side of following Jesus, my wife and I were asked by our church to either stop pursuing this new direction or to leave the fellowship so we would not cause division. They were not open to such things; they believed these were false signs and wonders done by the enemy and not through the Holy Spirit.

I hadn't been more excited and on fire for God in years. The choice to leave was quite easy. My prayers had been answered.

As a confirmation of our decision to leave, the Holy Spirit led me to lay hands on my seven-year-old son and command that he be healed in Jesus' name. He had suffered his whole life from celiac disease: a digestive disorder that severely limited his diet. The Bible promises that *"by his wounds we are healed"* (**Isaiah 53:5, 1 Peter 2:24**). As I was praying for his digestive system to be restored, I opened my eyes to see what he was doing. He was sitting up in his bed, his face and hands raised to heaven, eyes closed, smiling from ear to ear, just drinking it all in. He was completely and miraculously healed on the spot.

A few years later, a door opened up to attend the Kingdom Training School of Supernatural through Blazing Fire Church in Pleasanton, CA, where lay people like me could learn to walk out our faith in our true kingdom identity, bringing heaven to earth in the power and authority of Jesus. It was here that Pastor Brent Lokker introduced me to the real meaning of biblical grace. Given my many years of conflicting theology, I struggled to accept it. For every point he made, I knew several Scriptures that contradicted it.

He suggested I ask the Holy Spirit to teach me. I decided to put aside my preconceived ideas and let the Holy Spirit show me in His time. One day, He told me to look up some of these contradictory passages in Greek. As I dug into Scriptures that had once caused me to live in fear of not measuring up, He opened up my eyes to see them through the lenses of grace. The results are the following chapters.

CHAPTER 11:
ENDURE TO THE END

Mark 13:13 – (Jesus speaking) *"And everyone will hate you because you are my followers. But the one who endures to the end will be saved."*

Scratching the Surface

At first glance, this verse seems to say that if we remain faithful to Him and endure every trial or temptation, then we will be saved (i.e. go to heaven and not go to hell). It also seems to imply that if we don't endure, if we fall short and give into fear or some other temptation, then we will be lost (i.e. we will forfeit our salvation).

Law vs. Grace

I used to believe this surface meaning and would attempt to apply this unattainable standard to myself as well as to others who claimed to be Christians. I unknowingly put myself and others under the law with this Old Covenant thinking. This perspective imposes condemnation on anyone who doesn't obey perfectly. It draws a line in the sand and says that if we cross it, we will lose our salvation. Depending on what church or teaching we are under, this line is drawn at different levels of disobedience.

Some of us might say that if we have hidden sin in our lives, then we will not be saved; that by hiding our sin, we have not endured to the end. But what amount of hidden sin is too much? All of us have hidden sin to some degree. No one can totally confess all sin. If we tried, we would talk about nothing else, and even then we wouldn't be able to get it all out in the open.

Take lust for example. Could any of us really confess all of it? At what exact point does noticing that someone else is attractive to us become lust? Some of us think we know, but do we really? What if we see someone and we don't look too long but then later think about that person? How long is too long to think about them?

What about being discontented? Do any of us confess that as a sin? If we are driving an older car and see our dream car drive by and then think that we would really like to drive one of those one day, are we being ungrateful and discontent with what we have? At what point does this thinking become sin?

These types of questions go on and on when we attempt to measure up to a standard and put the focus of our salvation on our own level of righteousness or purity of heart instead of on what Jesus did for us. Paul says that if we try to meet an expectation in order to obtain or keep our salvation, then the cross is pointless.

> **Galatians 2:21** – *...if righteousness could be gained through the law, Christ died for nothing!*

We can't have it both ways. Either we are saved completely by what Jesus did or by how well we live up to the standard. Either Jesus paid for all sin on the cross or He didn't.

It's Greek to Me

The context of this passage is persecution: being hated for being a Christian and even being put to death for one's faith. To say that we *"will be saved"* refers to going to heaven does not make sense in this context. Jesus is not saying that when we are being persecuted we better not deny Him or we will lose our salvation and go to hell. That is just not the heart of Jesus we see in the gospels and it goes against the very definition of grace.

Peter gave into fear and denied Jesus three times in His darkest hour. He did not endure to the end, yet he was still saved. Or did Peter lose his salvation at that point only to regain it when Jesus reinstated him?

Do we go back and forth between being saved and lost depending on what we do or by how well we obey the Scriptures? If so, then we are actually saved by our own works and not by grace. We are saying that the result of our own obedience or disobedience is more powerful than the result of the cross. This thinking blatantly denies that Jesus paid for the sin of the entire world. If there is even one sin in our entire lives that resulted in our condemnation then we nullify the sacrifice Jesus made on the cross.

This word *saved* can also mean "to save a suffering one" or "to preserve one who is in danger"[28]. The context of this passage speaks more of Jesus rescuing us from suffering when we are persecuted than it does of us maintaining our salvation.

This is illustrated when we see Stephen praying while he's being stoned.

> **Acts 7:59-60** - *While they were stoning him, Stephen prayed, "Lord Jesus, receive my spirit." Then he fell on his knees and cried out, "Lord, do not hold this sin against them." When he had said this, he fell asleep.*

Apparently, Stephen is not feeling much pain at all while the Pharisees pummel him with stones. He should have been in agony as the rocks slammed into him, but instead he prays for his killers. He actually seems completely oblivious to the rocks. It appears that Jesus was somehow saving him from suffering the pain of being stoned for his faith.

When the Bible says *"he fell asleep,"* it doesn't mean he took a nap. This expression was how New Testament writers referred to dying. Since Jesus conquered death and said

John 11:26 – *"...whoever lives by believing in me will never die."*

they didn't want to contradict Him. Of course, Jesus is right; we don't really die. We pass on to eternal life, but culturally, in America, we still call it dying. Although, we also refer to it as passing away or passing on.

Going back to the passage in question, the phrase *"endures to the end"* does not mean to the end of our physical life, as in the case of Stephen. Since the context is persecution, it is referring to the end of the persecution against us. It doesn't have to be that we are being killed for our faith, it could be someone just making a derogatory comment about us because we are believers. Whatever it is, Jesus promises to preserve us as we hold on to Him through it.

The implication of the Greek word *endures* is "one that remains behind after others have gone" or "to keep one's ground in a conflict."[29] Jesus is saying that if we are the ones who remain behind and don't flee in fear from persecution, He will be with us and save us from suffering more than our faith can handle.

Found in Translation

To better understand the context and meaning of this passage, we could re-translate it to something like

"But the one who remains behind to face the persecution all the way through will be saved from suffering too much."

Being persecuted can be a frightening ordeal, no matter what form it takes. The temptation to give in to fear and flee from the situation can easily overwhelm us despite any previous victories we may have experienced.

Take Elijah for example. In 1 Kings 18, he challenged 950 false prophets of demon gods to a duel. The god who lit the sacrifice on fire was the real God. Their god failed, but our God came through with an amazing display of power. Shortly after putting all these false prophets to death, Elijah got death threats from Jezebel and he ran away in fear, praying that the Lord would kill him. Did this act of cowardice in the face of persecution cause Elijah to fall out of favor with God? Not at all. God came to him and encouraged him. Elijah then walked so closely with the Lord that he didn't even experience death. God just took him to heaven in a whirlwind.

Despite any failure in bravery or faith we may encounter when persecuted, Jesus understands the temptation to give into the fear. He knows how hard it is to remain behind and face the persecution all the way through, so when we do stick it out to the end, we can be completely confident that He will be right there with us all the way.

CHAPTER 12:
THE ROCKY SOIL

Mark 4:16-17 – (Jesus speaking) *"Others, like seed sown on rocky places, hear the word and at once receive it with joy. But since they have no root, they last only a short time. When trouble or persecution comes because of the word, they quickly fall away."*

Scratching the Surface

These verses are part of Jesus' explanation of a parable that He told earlier. The last sentence seems to indicate that if we are not rooted in what we believe, we will turn our backs on God when we suffer some challenges. It implies that if we are shallow in our faith, our knowledge, or our relationship with God, we will not last long as believers. Our faith will wither and die from the heat of persecution, thus forfeiting our salvation.

Law vs. Grace

Earlier in my Christian walk, I would shake my head and say, "What a shame," when people would excitedly become believers but then leave the church a few weeks or months later. In my belief system at that time, I equated leaving the church with losing salvation because of misinterpreting Scriptures like this one. My shallow, unspiritual doctrines would conclude that if Jesus was the head of the church and we were His body, when someone left the church, they would also cut off their connection with Jesus. Leaving the body meant leaving the head as well.

But the "church" encompasses all believers everywhere and not just those who are part of a formal organized group. Leaving **a** church is not synonymous to leaving **the** church. In fact, under grace, we can leave **a** church, but there is no such thing as leaving **the** church. As we discussed in Part II, once He is in us, there is no getting Him out, and once we are in Him, there is no getting us out. It's once and for all. Someone might go off on their own and try to run away from God, as well as from people, like in the parable of The Lost Son, but it's impossible to undo the relationship. Once a son, always a son. Once we are part of the church, we are always part of the church. Being in the church is the same as being in His family.

Law-based, Old Covenant thinking always wants to put limits on grace out of fear that we will abuse it. But it is the very fact that we can abuse it that wins us over. His kindness can lead us to repentance. God is not threatened or worried about us squandering our inheritance.

Law-focused people can also be overly worried about what others will think of the church if there are messed-up people in it. We can think that we must have it all together in order to impress the world or even other congregations and prove that God is with us, as opposed to us just accepting the fact that we are all messed up to varying degrees. Some of us aren't quite done messing up in big, ugly, disgraceful ways even though we have already said yes to Jesus. There should be no place more welcoming of really messed-up people than those who belong to the King of messed-up people.

All of the punishment for all of our mistakes has already been carried out on Jesus at the cross, so we can relax and work through our issues without having to worry about God getting mad at us or being disappointed in us if we trip up or get off track along the way. If God's grace is big enough to handle it, then ours should be as well.

We also don't have to feel pressured about how quickly we get back up or about how much progress we should be making. Oftentimes we can make the most progress by just being still and resting in His faithfulness and goodness. When we can rest in His unfailing, unconditional love and acceptance of us, we have a safe place to get healed from whatever wounds are causing us to act contrary to who we really are. As God heals us and makes us whole, we can start making more efforts to represent Christ to the world and become a walking testimony to His goodness and power.

None of us can really fall away from God, despite what this verse appears to be saying. The concept of falling away does not exist in the New Covenant. It is an impossibility by the definition of grace. That being so, what does this verse mean?

It's Greek to Me

Jesus is again speaking to His disciples about being persecuted. He is preparing them for what is coming. The word translated as "fall away" is the Greek root word *skandalizō* with a definition of "to lay a snare for, set a trap for; hence, to cause to stumble or fall, to give offence or scandal to anyone."[30]

In looking at Jesus' life, how did the religious leaders try to make trouble for Him? One way was to approach Him while He was teaching the crowds and ask Him a question designed to trap or ensnare Him into saying something against the law, thereby offending the people and discrediting Him.

Jesus is warning His followers to make sure that they are rooted in what they believe because opposers will try to do the same thing to them that they did to Him. Religious people will attempt to make us stumble or fall in order to create a scandal about us so that others will not listen. If we are rooted in the Word and in our relationship with the Holy Spirit, we will be able to answer wisely, as Jesus did, and avoid being discredited in front of others.

Found in Translation

Translating this word as "fall away" may be confusing to readers and opens the door for incorrect doctrinal conclusions that contradict the gospel of grace. Another way to write it that better captures the meaning and context of what Jesus was trying to say might be:

"When trouble or persecution comes because of the word, they are quickly scandalized."

Without being rooted, we will get tripped up by questions or debate tactics and we won't know how to answer in a way that is consistent with God's heart and His truth. We will become scandalized by the opposition, our credibility will be undermined, and we will lose influence with people who are looking for answers. Peter exhorts us to be ready.

> **1 Peter 3:15-16** – *But in your hearts revere Christ as Lord.* ***Always be prepared to give an answer to everyone*** *who asks you to give the reason for the hope that you have. But do this with gentleness and respect, keeping a clear conscience, so that those who speak maliciously against your good behavior in Christ may be ashamed of their slander.* (emphasis mine)

We get ourselves ready and root ourselves in Him by reading His Word through the lenses of grace and by listening to grace-filled messages. The more we understand grace, the more we sink our roots into His heart for us and for the world. The deeper our roots go, the stronger our faith will be. When opposition comes and tries to ensnare us or lead us astray, we will be able to see through the hollow deception of needing to measure up to receive or keep grace.

> **Colossians 2:6-8** – *So then, just as you received Christ Jesus as Lord, continue to live your lives in him,* ***rooted and built up in him, strengthened in the faith*** *as you were taught, and overflowing with thankfulness.*

> *See to it that no one takes you captive through hollow and deceptive philosophy, which depends on human tradition and the elemental spiritual forces of this world rather than on Christ.*

> (emphasis mine)

CHAPTER 13:
HOLD TO MY TEACHING

John 8:31-32 – *To the Jews who had believed him, Jesus said, "If you hold to my teaching, you are really my disciples. Then you will know the truth, and the truth will set you free."*

Scratching the Surface

On the surface, this verse seems to say that if we obey Jesus' teachings, we are really His followers. Thus, we can infer that if we are not obeying His teachings, we are not really Christians. In other words, obey or be condemned.

In my law-based days of Christianity, we would often use this verse in Bible studies with people who considered themselves believers. We would have them measure their obedience against the commands of Jesus. Of course, they would fail the test, and we jumped on the opportunity to lead them to the conclusion that they had never become a true disciple of Jesus. Then we would teach them the "biblical standards" of discipleship.

Jesus is talking to Jews who already believed in Him. He appears to be telling them that He does not consider them His disciples because they are not holding to His teaching. This implies that it takes more than belief to follow Jesus, to know the truth, and to be set free. We reasoned that because they weren't obeying His teachings, they didn't really know the truth and they weren't really set free.

This begs the questions, "How much obedience is enough to be or stay saved?" and "Where is the line that says we have disobeyed too much?"

The problem with this perspective is that it takes the focus of our salvation off the fact that Jesus was punished for all of our disobedience on the cross and puts it onto how well we are following His commands. This is an Old Covenant mindset that brings law into the New Covenant of grace.

Law vs. Grace

A law-based perspective will always have us examining ourselves to see if we are measuring up to some expectation. This expectation changes depending on who is setting it. It leaves us feeling insecure in our relationship with God and where we stand with Him. Are we obeying well enough to be accepted today? Or are we giving in to temptations and struggling to overcome, causing us to feel condemned and disappointing to Him?

We cannot satisfy the law with our obedience. The enemy is an expert lawyer and is always ready to accuse us of falling short. He will tell us that we might have done okay in one area but we still messed up in another. If we read our Bible for thirty minutes, he will tell us that if we really loved God, we would have read it for an hour. If we share our faith with someone, he will tell us that if we were really disciples of Jesus, we would have set up a Bible study with them. It is a neverending treadmill of trying to meet an arbitrary expectation that will always move just beyond what we do. This is one way the enemy attacks our identity and gets us sidetracked with perpetual striving. There is no rest here, nor is there any peace.

Should we do our best to obey the commands of Jesus? Absolutely! He gave them for a reason and, as His followers, it is our hearts' desire to be unified with His will for us in any given moment. But our motivation for obedience is not so that we won't be rejected or so that we won't get in trouble. This is a fear-based motive which always comes from being under the law. Under grace, our motivation for obeying is out of love, gratitude, desire for intimacy, etc., and not a threat of punishment.

Those of us under the law will say that our motivation is also love, gratitude, and desire for intimacy, but because there is also the threat of rejection for not meeting the standard, it muddies the otherwise clear waters. It sours the sauce. As mentioned before

> **Galatians 5:9** – "*A little yeast works through the whole batch of dough.*"

It doesn't matter if we are 99 percent grace and 1 percent law, the results are the same. The law will eventually worm its way into everything, tainting our hearts with its demands of performance and its fear of punishment. It must be 100% grace. 100% Jesus. 100% saved. **If there is any possibility of us losing our salvation, then Jesus did not pay for every sin on the cross.** This simply goes against the entire point of the cross. Either Jesus was punished for all sin, for all people, for all time, or He wasn't. If He was, then we can shout for joy because we are the most blessed people on earth. If He wasn't, then we are cursed with the burden of always striving to fulfill the law. Which one sounds like good news?

It's Greek to Me

Back to the passage at hand. The Greek word for *hold* in "*hold to His teachings*" is translated differently in other Bible versions. The more common translations include "abide in," "continue in," or "remain in,"[31] and it does not mean "obey." It means to stay or live in a certain place, or to make a home or dwell somewhere.

This same word is used about forty times in the book of John and nowhere else is it translated as *hold*. The vast majority of the time it is translated as either "remain" or "stay."

The context of these verses is that Jesus is talking to Jews. Jesus was emphasizing that they remain with His Word because they were brought up learning the law and He was bringing a radical departure from what they were used to. He was stressing that they needed to make their new home in the fact that He was the Savior, the Son of God who had come to rescue them. They already believed it, but they needed to stay in that place of belief because He was going to the cross, and, because of that, their belief would be tested.

They weren't expecting a crucified Savior. They were expecting a Messiah who would lead a military rebellion against the Romans. So when they would see Jesus hanging on a cross, they would undoubtedly be confused. But He promised that if they held on to their belief in Him, they would know the truth about why He had to be crucified, and then they could be set free from the law (i.e. set free from sin).

Jesus told them earlier that belief in Him was the only thing they needed to work at.

> **John 6:28-29** – *Then they asked him, "What must we do to do the works God requires?"*

> *Jesus answered, "The work of God is this: to believe in the one he has sent."*

The Jews had been in a works-based system for many centuries, so moving to a grace-based system would not make sense until Jesus sent the Holy Spirit to teach them what it all meant. It was a huge shift to go from "do, do, do" to "done, done, done." To go from "work to be good enough" and "strive to be accepted" to having faith in a Savior who says,

Matthew 11:28 – *"Come to me, all you who are weary and burdened, and I will give you rest."*

Found in Translation

Using *hold* instead of "abide," "continue," or "remain" caused some Christians to form some serious doctrinal errors that brought accusation and condemnation into other believers' lives. Instead of looking at Jesus' teachings through the finished work of the cross and the grace it purchased, they were led by the enemy into establishing a law-based, works-oriented standard of what makes a disciple of Jesus.

The New American Standard Bible translates the verse more clearly

"If you continue in My word, then you are truly disciples of Mine..."

The *word* that Jesus is referring to is that He is the Christ, the Messiah, the Savior of the world. It is the only *word* that matters. By putting our faith in Jesus to save us, we are truly His disciples.

CHAPTER 14:
THE TRUE VINE

John 15:1-2 – *"I am the true vine, and my Father is the gardener. He cuts off every branch in me that bears no fruit, while every branch that does bear fruit he prunes so that it will be even more fruitful."*

Scratching the Surface

This passage seems to say that unless we are actively sharing the gospel and converting the lost, we will be cut off from Jesus. And that even if we are bearing fruit, we can expect Him to strip us of anything that might be getting in the way of us being more effective. While God is passionate for the lost to be saved, as we all should be, is He really a slave-driving dictator who is holding pruning shears over our head, ready to clip us from the vine unless we meet our fruit quota?

Law vs. Grace

In my years under the burden of the law, this was a very scary Scripture. I often wondered how much fruit was enough to not get cut off of the vine. I mean, sure I could share my faith with people, but I didn't really have control over whether or not they became Christians. Verses like these produced a lot of pressure in my life and every so often I felt the need to escape. Rebellion would rise up in me and sin would seize the opportunity.

> **Romans 7:8** – *But sin, seizing the opportunity afforded by the commandment, produced in me every kind of coveting. For apart from the law, sin was dead.*

Constantly being under the pressure of trying to measure up to the commandments kicks the door wide open for sin to go wild. When we are burdened with always having to meet certain expectations or else be rejected, we can only take so much. Some might say that this is just part of life, and I would agree that it is a **part** of life. It does need to be part of our work life and our school life to a certain extent, but it can't be part of our closest, most intimate relationships. If we don't have a relationship with God and with at least a few key people where we feel completely accepted and loved just as we are, then we will always be insecure and feel a burden to try to be good enough.

The curse of needing to meet some standard is not only applicable in our relationship with God, it also applies to parents, spouses, siblings, friends, etc. When we feel a threat of rejection in any of these key relationships, the same thing happens that Paul speaks of above. Sin will seize that opportunity and we will either be overwhelmed with desires to escape or we will become self-righteous from our persistent efforts. For example, when parents are overly protective, overly strict, or set unattainable expectations, it can embitter the child and stir their desire to rebel. This can eventually lead them to give up on trying any further since they feel they are doomed to fail. On the other hand, if they persevere in their striving for acceptance and approval it can move them toward being self-righteous toward anyone not trying as hard as they are.

Las Vegas has made a fortune on focusing their marketing to those of us who choose the route of rebellion. Their current slogan "What happens in Vegas, stays in Vegas" even encourages us to lie about how we escape and indulge.

The enemy wants us under law in as many areas of our lives as possible because when there is a standard we must try to meet he can accuse us of being a failure or tempt us into judging others for their failures. If we find ourselves consistently struggling with judging others or with certain sins, we must ask the Holy Spirit where we feel like we are not measuring up or being good enough. As said before, it is in this area of our life where Daddy wants to upgrade our thinking and teach us how to see ourselves from His perspective.

Grace lifts us above the law where we walk on higher paths, hand-in-hand with the Lover of our souls. Grace takes us to a place of complete safety and security, where we can curl up in our Daddy's lap and let Him hug us tight, knowing we are totally accepted, even celebrated, just the way we are. As the Scripture above says, when there is no law, sin is dead. Sin loses most of its appeal when we are embraced by unconditional love. The more we experience how much we are loved and cherished in our current state, the less attractive temptations become.

> **Titus 2:11-12** - *For the grace of God...teaches us to say "No" to ungodliness and worldly passions, and to live self-controlled, upright and godly lives...*

Grace is always the solution to a sin problem. We can't shame our way into holy living. Grace promotes security. Shame promotes fear. Grace empowers us with freedom. Shame shackles us with oppression.

It's Greek to Me

To have Jesus threaten His followers with cutting them off from Him if they fail in some way is not consistent with His heart of grace. The Greek root word for *cuts off* is *airō* and means the following: "to take up, lift up, raise up; to take up and carry away, take away."[32] Several Bibles choose to translate it as *take away* because it seems to be what Jesus is trying to say. But "lift up" or "raise up" agrees with horticultural practices. It also agrees more with the grace of the New Covenant.

When we are not living in ways that are consistent with who He says we are, that is, not acting like sons and daughters, kings and queens, priests and priestesses, we will not be fruitful. We are being distracted with things of the world and giving into temptations to escape into unhealthy things. With his accusations and condemnations, the enemy pulls us down from the high place of grace and keeps us on the ground, eating the dust of sin.

> **Genesis 3:14** – (God speaking to Satan) *"You will crawl on your belly and you will eat dust all the days of your life."*

When growing grapes, if a branch is on the ground (eating dust) it will not produce fruit, so the gardener lifts it up and loops it through the other branches to keep it out of the dirt. This a beautiful picture of what we need when we are wallowing in sin. We need Jesus to lift us up out of the dust, remind us of who we are, and re-insert us into the fellowship of grace-filled believers. He doesn't cut us off because we give in to the enemy's deception and mistakenly put ourselves back under law. That goes against His nature of patience and faithfulness. Instead, if we are willing, He lifts us back up to our rightful spot with Him, above condemnation for sin, where we will effortlessly produce fruit through the love and grace He showers on us.

In regard to the fruitful branch, the Greek word translated *prunes* literally means "to cleanse from filth." This is also an accurate description of what a grape grower does. When a branch is producing fruit, it is washed with water to remove any insects, debris, etc., so that it can grow its fruit totally unhindered. That's how Jesus is with us. He says, "Great job! What you are doing is very valuable and makes a huge difference. Keep up the good work."

When we are walking in our true identity, releasing the glories of the kingdom into people's lives, and overflowing with fruit, Jesus doesn't prune us. Instead, He washes us with His words of approval and encouragement so that we will be even more fruitful.

> **Ephesians 5:26** – *Christ loved the church and gave himself up for her to make her holy, cleansing (or having cleansed) her by the washing with water through the word...*" (brackets mine)

In the very next sentence of John 15, Jesus confirms that He is talking about cleansing.

> **John 15:3** – *"You are already clean because of the word I have spoken to you."*

This word for *clean* is the same root word as what is being translated as *prunes* in the previous verse. In fact, it's the same root word as *cleansing* from the verse in Ephesians. *Prunes* just doesn't convey the heart of grace that Jesus has for us and how He continually washes us with His words of affirmation when we are bearing the fruit He desires.

There are certainly times in our lives where we get pruned as well, but that is not how the word is used here.

Found in Translation

When we read the Bible with the lenses of grace, we will weed out the law. These lenses will expose the law for being the fraud that it is when it is being presented in the wrong context. If there are Scriptures intended to be looked at in a New Covenant context, yet they seem to offer up the threat of condemnation, it is the enemy attempting to insert the law back into our lives.

> **Romans 8:1** – *...there is now no condemnation for those who are in Christ Jesus...*

There is never any condemnation for us. Not when we are indulging in sin. Not when we produce too little fruit. Not when we fail to share our faith with a certain number of people. Not when we don't sacrifice enough time or money to the needy. Not ever.

There is no condemnation for us *now*. Right now. No matter what we are doing or how we are doing because we are in Christ Jesus.

A possible grace-filled translation of the passage in question could be the following

> "I am the true vine and my Father is the vine grower. Every branch in me that does not bring forth fruit, He lifts up. Every branch that does bring forth fruit, He cleans so that it will bring forth fruit in greater quantity and quality."

When we live and grow in a spiritual environment of peace and security, knowing that we are completely loved, accepted, and celebrated by Him, we can't help but overflow with joy and produce fruit. It's just a natural result of being lifted up out of the dust and dwelling in the higher place of grace.

CHAPTER 15:
FORGIVING OTHERS

Matthew 6:14-15 – (Jesus speaking) *"For if you forgive men when they sin against you, your heavenly Father will also forgive you. But if you do not forgive men their sins, your Father will not forgive your sins."*

Scratching the Surface

The point Jesus is making seems abundantly clear. If we forgive others, we will be forgiven by God. If we don't, we won't. Simple, right?

Simple but scary. How do we know when we have truly forgiven someone? We can say we forgive, but if we still have heightened emotions concerning that person, have we really let it go? Must we scour our memory to find anyone and everyone who has ever wronged us, and then tell our heavenly Father that we forgive each person by name? Or do we need to track them down and tell them ourselves? Can we just make a blanket statement in our hearts that we forgive everyone who has ever hurt us? How can we know for sure if we have forgiven everyone and have done so to an acceptable level?

Law vs. Grace

Hopefully by now this line of questioning causes our "law alarm" to go off. We should be able to recognize that when something tells us we must meet certain criteria in order to qualify for salvation, the enemy is using the law to veil our eyes and blind us to grace. His only weapon is deception, and if he can get us to agree with his deception then we invite him to have more influence over our thinking. He will take the text out of context in order to con us.

We typiclly love to be in control and fix our own problems. Overcoming difficulties and challenges by focusing our attention on finding solutions and working hard gives us a sense of validation and satisfaction. That's why the law is so appealing to us and why it's so easy for us to be deceived by it. It tells us that if we would only pray more, if we would only repent of this sin, if we would only obey this Scripture, then everything would fall into place. But it never ends. There will always be another, "if we would only..." for us to "do" so God will be pleased or we will get a breakthrough or overcome some sin. In this case, if only we would forgive, we would be forgiven.

In our humanity, we love to have our success be a result of our own effort. In God's wisdom, He flipped the playing field so that the least would be the greatest. Those of us who were some of the biggest failures in life tend to have a much easier time receiving grace and thriving in it. Those of us who were very successful by our hard work and sacrifice can have the hardest time letting go of the law.

When we hold on to the law, our focus is on our own obedience, our own humility, our own openness, our own sacrifice, our own love, the condition of our own heart, etc. and how all of these things make us close to God or right with God. The fact is, focusing on these things only perpetuates the endless treadmill of trying to achieve our own righteousness and holiness.

Under the law, we don't want to accept the fact that salvation, righteousness, and holiness are gifts because we think it cheapens them and people will take advantage of them. We like having to work hard to be successful because we feel it sets us apart from those who are unwilling to do what it takes to overcome. It's how we get our sense of identity and worth.

As law-bound believers, we wrap up who we are in how we perform and we put our security in our success or failure. This paradigm makes sense to us. We like the idea of grace but only under the context of law, meaning that our faith causes us to obey the commands and that qualifies us for grace. The idea that we must view the law under the context of grace is foreign, meaning that we receive salvation as a gift of grace, and only then does it cause us to obey the law.

It is only in letting go of what we understand (i.e. law-based living) and letting God lift the veil in due time, that we will get the revelation of grace. Which, by the way, is the gospel.

> **Galatians 1:6-7** – *I am astonished that you are so quickly deserting the one who called you to live in* **the grace of Christ** *and are turning to a different gospel—which is really no gospel at all.* (emphasis mine)

The only true gospel is *"the grace of Christ."* Anything else is *"no gospel at all."* Grace is not theology. Grace is the gospel. It is the good news. Anything else is not the New Covenant.

It's Greek to Me

There isn't any problem with how this passage is translated. The only issue here is making sure we keep the text in context. Jesus is expressing an Old Covenant teaching in an Old Covenant setting.

Because Jesus lived under the Old Covenant, He had to obey the law perfectly in order to fulfill it. He also had to teach others to uphold and obey the law. He would not have upheld the law if He taught people to break it.

Starting in Matthew 5, Jesus preached a long sermon on the law, but He didn't just reiterate what the Jews knew to be the law. He pulled back the curtain and revealed the true extent of the law, just how high the bar was really set. In doing so, He exposed the fact that we cannot measure up to it, that it was a burden too heavy for us to bear and a yoke too hard for us to pull.

Even though it was Jesus who was speaking, He was not laying out the gospel of the New Covenant. From Matthew 5:1 until Matthew 7:29, Jesus spelled out the commands of the law in greater depth and with more wisdom than the people had ever heard before. They were completely gripped by His words, His presence, His authority. He opened up their understanding and inspired them to do their best to obey the law with pure hearts, as a good spiritual leader under the Old Covenant should do.

Right after He taught them how to pray, He spoke the words we are focusing on here, and they are classic law. The law always says, "If you do this or don't do that, then you will be considered righteous."

Under grace, much of the law still applies, but the issue of our salvation is no longer on the table. Our righteousness in God's eyes is not part of the equation anymore. Under grace, Jesus has already paid the penalty for all of our sins, mistakes, shortcomings, weaknesses, etc., so our salvation is completely secure—our righteousness before God is eternal. However, also under grace, the principles of the law are still true. **We will be rewarded or disciplined based on our obedience, not only to the law, but also to New Testament commands and to the instructions of His voice.**

Found in Translation

Under the New Covenant, we do not have to forgive others in order to be forgiven by our heavenly Father. We are forgiven by God based on what Jesus did for us. His blood washed away everything that needed to be forgiven or ever will need to be forgiven. Our forgiveness is not based on anything we do or don't do. It is based on the cross paying our debt. It is a gift of grace. Undeserved. Unearned.

Plus, to make things even more clear, this Old Covenant verse in Matthew has been directly superseded by a New Covenant verse.

Colossians 3:13 – ...*Forgive as the Lord forgave you.*

We forgive because we have already been forgiven, not in order to receive forgiveness. We give grace as freely as it has been given to us. God has completely forgiven and forgotten our transgressions. He does not keep a record of our mistakes and, as such, we should do the same with others. It is our job to be like Him as much as we can, so people inside the church and outside can experience the transforming power of grace.

CHAPTER 16:
CANNOT BE MY DISCIPLE

Luke 14:25-27 – *Large crowds were traveling with Jesus, and turning to them he said: "If anyone comes to me and does not hate father and mother, wife and children, brothers and sisters—yes, even their own life—such a person cannot be my disciple. And whoever does not carry their cross and follow me cannot be my disciple.*

Luke 14:33 – (Jesus speaking) *"...any of you who does not give up everything he has cannot be my disciple."*

Scratching the Surface

Throughout the Gospels, Jesus sprinkles in what seem to be qualifications to follow Him and these look pretty daunting. Hate our father and mother? Carry our cross? Give up everything? What does He mean? It sounds like unless we walk away from our family, friends, job, material possessions, etc., we are disqualified from being a disciple of Jesus, that we cannot be saved. Wow! Could this be true? Is this consistent with the New Covenant of grace?

Law vs. Grace

We used this impossibly high expectation in my measure-up-or-else church to weed out those who were not willing to be sold out in following Jesus. If people were unwilling to live up to these standards, they could not become a Christian and be saved. It seems pretty harsh but, in our minds, it was the expectation Jesus set not us. We were just trying to follow the Bible and restore Jesus' standards so that the church could be what it was meant to be.

We also brought these standards back up to those in our fellowship who seemed to be slipping or, worse yet, to those who resisted any instruction or direction that our ministry leaders set out. For example, if the leadership decided that the church was going to give a special contribution to support missions or some other project, everyone was expected to wholeheartedly get on board and cheerfully give their pre-determined amount. If we didn't have the extra money, then we needed to come up with ways to raise the money.

Along the way, the church leaders checked up on us to see how much money we had on hand. If we were behind then we would be asked something like, "What's going on in your heart, bro?" or "How are you doing in your relationship with God?" They assumed our efforts were lacking because we were struggling with sin.

This is just one example of how everyone in the church was expected to completely get on board in the name of unity, and if we didn't, our hearts needed "discipling." This was a made-up term for correcting, training, or even rebuking each other in order to keep our hearts soft toward God and His church.

With the help of this passage and others like it, we concluded that the biblical standard for being a true disciple of Jesus was someone who was willing to give up everything, go anywhere, and do anything for the kingdom (a.k.a. the church). Again, we were just trying to follow what we thought the Bible laid out. It might sound very controlling and legalistic, almost cult-like, but we were sincere in our faith and in our efforts to be close to God. We wanted to show our love for Him through our obedience and humility.

The problem with this perspective is that it is completely law-based. Our salvation was based on whether we lived up to the standard that Jesus set. Is living up to a standard how we obtain forgiveness and righteousness in the New Covenant? Or does this sound like Old Covenant thinking?

If this is Old Covenant thinking, how do we reconcile the fact that Jesus said it to anyone who wants to be His disciple?

It's Greek to Me

This passage, including the others like it where Jesus says we must do such-and-such or else we cannot be His disciples, are being misinterpreted because of the translation of one word. When Jesus says we *cannot* be His disciples, He is not saying that we are disqualified or disallowed if we do not meet His standards.

The Greek word in question is *dunamai*, which means "to be able, to have power."[33] It does not mean "to be allowed or to be qualified." But this is how we read it in our culture. When Jesus says that unless we do something we cannot be His disciples, we take it to mean that we are not allowed to be His disciples because we are not meeting His criteria. This is not at all what Jesus means. Even though translating this word as *cannot* is technically correct, it is culturally incorrect for us and leads us to misinterpret what Jesus is saying, thereby leading us to create wrong doctrines.

A better translation would be that we are not able or do not have the power to be His disciples, as in Young's Literal Translation:

> "So, then, every one of you who doth not take leave of all that he himself hath, **is not able to be my disciple.**"

Although, this also has a chance of being misunderstood in the same way, it is not as blatant as *cannot*. We could still read it to mean that we are being disqualified. What Jesus meant was that we will not have the power to be His disciples. In other words, **when we do not let go of all that we have in this world, we will not have the power to live as Jesus did.**

This completely changes the passage and brings it in line with the grace we find in the New Covenant. It is not a mandatory requirement of salvation for us to meet this "standard." Instead, we find a biblical principle at work that we also find in other passages; the more we free ourselves of the world, the more we are empowered to walk in Jesus' footsteps.

Found in Translation

To make this and similar passages more clear to us so that we will not fall prey to the enemy's tricks to put us under the law, let's translate this word in a way that's consistent with grace.

> **Luke 14:25-27** – *Large crowds were traveling with Jesus, and turning to them he said: "If anyone comes to me and does not hate father and mother, wife and children, brothers and sisters—yes, even their own life—such a person* **will not have the power to** *be my disciple. And whoever does not carry their cross and follow me* **will not have the power to** *be my disciple.*

> **Luke 14:33** – *"...any of you who does not give up everything he has* **will not have the power to** *be my disciple."*

In this way, we capture the intent of His message and do not add a law-based burden to our lives through misinterpreting a less-than-optimal translation of a key word.

If we desire more power to walk as Jesus did, let us deny ourselves of distracting worldly passions, put our relationship with Jesus above every other relationship, and follow His example of how to minister.

CHAPTER 17:
LIFE AND DOCTRINE

1 Timothy 4:16 – *Watch your life and doctrine closely. Persevere in them, because if you do, you will save both yourself and your hearers.*

Scratching the Surface

This verse appears to imply that if we don't watch our life and doctrine closely, that is, how we live our lives and what we believe, as well as persevere in them, we will not save ourselves nor those whom we influence. It seems to indicate that we will not only lose our own salvation but also jeopardize the salvation of others if we fail to live up to a certain standard or if we have doctrinal misunderstandings.

So what does it mean to watch our life and doctrine closely? How closely do we have to watch them? How much perseverance is necessary? What part of our doctrine might disqualify us from salvation if we misunderstand it? How big or small of a mistake in our life or doctrine does it take to lose our salvation?

Law vs. Grace

If grace is undeserved favor, aren't we still undeserving when we mess up?
Or is it possible to be too undeserving to receive undeserved favor? Does that
even make sense?

It's unfortunate that we have to ask such a question, but that is what religion
does. It veils us from the obvious truth by keeping us stuck in an Old Covenant
mindset. Even Christians can be veiled from the very basis of the Good News,
the grace of Christ, just as the Jews were in the first century. Some of us will
accept the fact that Jesus is the Son of God, that He died for our sins, and rose
again on the third day, but then struggle with what "He died for our sins"
really means. We can still get caught up in thinking we need to qualify in
order for His sacrifice to apply to us. This is the veil of the law.

I used to use this verse to challenge people who said they were Christians, but
whom I believed were not, by getting them to examine how they were living
and what they believed. The intent was to get them to see that not only were
they not living up to the standards of a Christian but that they didn't even know
what the standards of being a Christian were. I would want them to come to the
conclusion that they never really became Christians because they never truly
repented of their sins. I also wanted them to see that their doctrine was way off
from what the Bible *really* taught. That way I could teach them what my church
believed to be sound doctrine regarding what it really meant to be a disciple of
Jesus. Then, according to this verse, they could effectively watch their life and
doctrine closely so that both they and their hearers could be saved.

However, thinking that how we live and what we believe (apart from Jesus
being our Savior) would determine whether or not we are still saved reveals
that we don't know what grace really means. It shows that we are out of touch
with the finished work of the cross: the fact that Jesus took ALL of our sin on
the cross, not just the sin we have confessed or repented of. It indicates that
the enemy has deceived us into thinking that our salvation is partially based
on our own obedience instead of being entirely based on faith in what Jesus
did for us.

Being under the law creates in us a judgmental attitude toward anyone who isn't at least trying to live up to the standard we think the Bible teaches. It also leads us to condemn anyone who doesn't believe the same doctrine we believe. It sets us up to live in judgment of everyone who says they are Christians but are not a part of our group. It splinters and divides the Body of Christ instead of drawing us together by our mutual joy over what Jesus actually accomplished for us.

Under grace we can experience true peace and rest, not only with God but with everyone, because we can see them through the grace lenses that God sees us through. Since our Heavenly Daddy completely accepts us just the way we are, we can in turn let others get a taste of unconditional acceptance by how we treat them. This is the love that the world hungers for. This is the longing of people's hearts. Everyone wants to be loved, accepted, and celebrated unconditionally. Only grace can do that.

It's Greek to Me

When we look at this entire passage in the Greek, the tone and implication of the original meaning has been changed in its translation. "*Watch your life and doctrine closely*" sounds like Paul is issuing Timothy a warning. It seems like he's saying, "Watch out!" as if something is about to hurt him, when the literal translation is "hold on to" or "pay attention to," which is more like general instruction. It's not hard to see how the translators got *watch* from "pay attention to," but in our culture it slightly changes the tone of the verse.

Also, the word translated *persevere* implies overcoming opposition. The literal Greek word means "continue with" or "remain with" which is more like walking along together hand in hand. Again, it's easy to see how translators got there because sometimes to "continue with" something means to "stick with it" which does conjure up notions of perseverance. Again, using *persevere* instead of *remain* slightly changes the implied meaning from instruction to warning, setting us up to make incorrect doctrinal conclusions.

It's ironic that a verse telling us to watch our doctrine closely is leading us away from sound doctrine.

The Greek root word for "save" is *sozo*. We typically only associate *save* with salvation, that is, with going to heaven. So when we see a verse that says if we don't do something then we won't be saved, we automatically think that losing our salvation is not only possible but, reasonably probable. As we have seen, this word has other meanings besides saving us from condemnation.

For Bible translators to use *save* in this context reveals that they did not make enough of an effort to have the verse be consistent with what Jesus did for us. If how we live and what we believe could cause us to lose our salvation, then we are not saved by grace but by our works. Grace means that our debt has been completely paid for us and not paid by us. Grace means that God did for us what we could not do for ourselves, and the only requirement or standard that we need to measure up to is to say yes to receiving His gift of salvation and to Jesus being Lord of our lives.

The idea of losing our salvation does not exist under grace. Since there is no such thing as losing our salvation, any verse that suggests that it is possible is being mistranslated or misinterpreted. In the case of this verse, the word *sozo* is mistranslated because it cannot mean "save" in terms of salvation and still line up with what grace means.

What is more alarming about the word *sozo* being translated as "save" in most translations is the implication that we will save ourselves and those who listen to us. Can we save ourselves? Can we save others? When did we become saviors? The idea that salvation for ourselves and others is up to how we live and what we teach puts us back under the law striving to measure up, so we can qualify for salvation. It is a works-based, Old Covenant way of thinking.

The tense of this Greek word is future active. *Future* obviously means it is something that hasn't happened yet. But Paul is talking to Timothy here, who was clearly already saved at this point. *Active* means that it is an action that Timothy initiates as opposed to something that happens to him. However, salvation is a God action in our lives and is not something that we do. So Paul cannot be saying that we will save ourselves by continuing to watch our lives and doctrine closely. It simply doesn't match with how the word is used here and it shows how much Old Testament works-based theology the church has allowed to infiltrate New Testament grace theology. It can't be both! If it's a mixture of works and grace then Jesus died for nothing because that is still Old Covenant.

The other potential meanings for *sozo* include "to preserve from danger,"[34] "to be healed," "to be delivered," and "to be made whole." In the context of this verse, where Paul is instructing Timothy on how to effectively lead and be an example to the believers, three out of these four definitions would make sense.

- **To preserve from danger:** this could apply in the sense that if Timothy holds on to the way he is currently living and the things he is currently teaching, he will be preserved from the danger of being corrupted by the world or by false teachings.

- **To be delivered:** this could apply in the same way as "to preserve from danger." He would be delivered from corruption or deception.

- **To be made whole:** this could work as well because by holding on to his current lifestyle and his current teaching, he would become whole, that is, all that God destined him to be.

How whole we become is completely up to us, and this fits well with the future active tense of the word. The more we obey the Word and the Spirit, the more intimacy with God we will experience, the more authority we will walk in, the more power will flow through us, the more impact we will make, the more character we will develop, the more resources He can trust us with, etc. That's what it means to be made whole. We will continue to uncover more and more of our true identity and be able to live out our divine destiny.

Found in Translation

One translation that would be more in line with the intent of the verse could be something like:

> "Hold on to how you are living and what you are teaching. Continue in them. In doing this, both you and those who hear you will be made whole."

Not only is the verse now consistent with the grace of the New Covenant, it also has a much softer tone. Instead of frightening us into right living so we can escape condemnation, it inspires us to become all that we were made to be, and to do so in the security of His unconditional and unfailing love.

CHAPTER 18:
SAME JUDGMENT AS THE DEVIL

1 Timothy 3:6 – *He must not be a recent convert, or he may become conceited and fall under the same judgment as the devil.*

Scratching the Surface

In this verse, Paul was writing to Timothy about how to set up church leadership in Ephesus. He was referring to the office of an overseer (a.k.a. bishop or elder) and what qualifications they needed to meet in order to be considered for the position. If they were too new of a believer, they could *"become conceited and fall under the same judgment as the devil."*

Whoa! That's a pretty heavy downside to becoming an overseer. Not many of us would volunteer for that position.

It's ironic to have someone who is doing well enough in their walk with the Lord to be considered for a key leadership role in the church, yet if they are too new in the faith, they could wind up being condemned with Satan to the burning lake of sulfur! What?!

Again, the questions start. How new of a convert is too new? How much pride or conceit would cause us to be condemned with the devil? Would we have time to repent or would we not find out we were condemned until it was too late?

Law vs. Grace

This is very inconsistent with the grace of Christ. If we were to fall under the same judgment as the devil for something as common and as immeasurable as conceit or pride, then we are all in danger of hell fire. We could never feel confident of our salvation and be able to boldly approach the throne of grace because we would need to constantly examine ourselves for too much pride.

While it is true that

James 4:6 – *"God opposes the proud and gives grace to the humble…"*

this verse in James is highlighting the difference between those who are in the world, that is, too proud to surrender to God's love, and those who have submitted to the Lordship of Jesus, humbly accepting Him as their Savior. Once we come to Jesus, we are completely covered by grace. Even our pride and conceit is covered by grace. If it weren't, we would all fail and be condemned.

God could certainly still oppose us after we were saved but only under the context of grace. In our pride we can all do things that God doesn't want us to do. He opposes us when we stubbornly do what is not His will. But He still lets us make our own choices and, if necessary, suffer some painful consequences.

Hebrews 12:5b-6 – *"My child, don't make light of the Lord's discipline, and don't give up when he corrects you. For the Lord disciplines those he loves, and he punishes each one he accepts as his child."* (NLT)

He disciplines us out of His great love, training us to trust that He knows what is best. When He lovingly disciplines us, it equates to Him opposing our pride within the context of grace.

The idea that we have to measure up to some unspecified level of humility in order to maintain our salvation would be reason for us to walk on eggshells in our relationship with Him. It would also be reason for us to pass judgment on anyone who exceeds what we think is the allowable amount of pride. When our salvation is measured by how we are doing, we start drawing lines and taking on God's role of separating the sheep and the goats, deciding who is lost and who is saved. But God says

James 4:12 – *...who are you to judge your neighbor?*

Romans 14:4 – *Who are you to judge someone else's servant? To their own master, servants stand or fall. And they will stand, for the Lord is able to make them stand.*

It is not our job to judge whether someone is lost or saved. It's also not our job to judge how well or poorly someone is doing in their walk. We must all follow our own path. It is the Lord who will make us stand, not one another handing out warnings of God's wrath coming upon the disobedient. (This is not to say we shouldn't counsel, correct, teach, admonish, etc., one another out of brotherly love.)

Until we see that grace completely covers us and all of our wrongdoing, we will continue to live in judgment of ourselves and others, missing out on the freedom and peace that Jesus purchased for us.

It's Greek to Me

In this same vein of judging others, Paul warned Timothy about appointing a new convert as an overseer. There are some interesting things to note with regard to this verse. Looking at Young's Literal Translation (YLT), we see some immediate differences from the NIV above.

1 Timothy 3:6 – *...not a new convert, lest having been puffed up he may fall to a judgment of the devil...*

In light of the YLT, the surface meaning of the overseer being condemned along with the devil can now be looked at from a different perspective. If the overseer is a new convert, he could become puffed up with self-importance and **start making judgments and accusations like the devil does.**

When we gain power or position that is beyond our maturity, we can start thinking we are better than others, ultimately making us more insecure because we have turned our focus onto ourselves. When pressure mounts and challenges come to us in this leadership role, we can start overreacting with slanderous accusations toward people who challenge or question our decisions.

We see an example of this when Jesus healed a man who was born blind. The man was later accused by the Pharisees of being *"steeped in sin at birth"* because he challenged their negative opinion of Jesus. They didn't have a good explanation for why Jesus could perform such miracles but still not be from God, so they insulted the man and kicked him out. (See John 9.)

As insecure people, we can sometimes launch a personal attack against those who challenge us in order to deflect the attention away from us and put the focus on some deficiency in the other person's life. Paul wanted to protect immature believers from being put in such a situation, so he gave Timothy very detailed instructions on how to select someone for the position.

In turning back to the YLT, the Greek word for *to* in *"may fall to a judgment of the devil"* is more commonly translated *into* which fits better in this instance. Now it becomes "may fall into a judgment of the devil."

Found in Translation

Incorporating what we've discussed above, one possible translation for this verse could be

> "...not a new convert, so he will not become conceited and fall into a judgment of the devil."

The meaning of the verse then goes from someone losing their salvation for becoming conceited, which does not fit with grace, to someone making a slanderous judgment like the devil would, which does fit with grace. When we become conceited, we start slandering others out of insecurity in order to exalt or protect ourselves. Slander and accusations are what the devil specializes in, so we would be allowing him to use us in this way. Paul's desire was to protect a newer believer from coming under this type of influence from the enemy.

CHAPTER 19:
BELIEVED IN VAIN

1 Corinthians 15:2 – *By this gospel you are saved, if you hold firmly to the word I preached to you. Otherwise, you have believed in vain.*

Scratching the Surface

This passage appears to say that if we do not *"hold firmly to the word"* then we *"have believed in vain."* In other words, we will forfeit our salvation if we don't keep believing or putting the word into practice.

But what does it mean to hold firmly to the word? How firmly do we have to hold to it in order to stay saved? What does he mean by *"this gospel"*?

Law vs. Grace

The gospel that Paul preached is actually summarized in the very next two verses. Paul taught

1 Corinthians 15:3-4 – *that Christ died for our sins according to the Scriptures, that he was buried, that he was raised on the third day according to the Scriptures,*

and that's it. He taught that if we put our trust in what Jesus did for us and stopped trying to be good enough, then the price He paid on our behalf would be credited to us. It's only when we think we have to do something more than just receive His gift that we become like the Galatian church and go from the joy of peace and freedom to the burden of the law.

Galatians 5:1 – *It is for freedom that Christ has set us free. Stand firm, then, and do not let yourselves be burdened again by a yoke of slavery [to the law]. (brackets mine)*

In my previous, law-bound church, we thought we were the ones who were free because we were working hard at overcoming sin and temptation. We had no idea that trying to maintain our salvation through our obedience to the Scriptures actually burdened us *"by a yoke of slavery"* to the law, empowering the very thing we were fighting so hard against. What we focus on grows. We chose to focus on the sin in our lives and how to be victorious over it through prayer, self-denial, and openness. Yet the more we focused on it, the more bound by the law we became. The grace that Paul preached, where we *"fix our eyes on Jesus"*[35] and what He did for us, wasn't something that had practical application.

And just where did Paul get his message of grace?

Galatians 1:11-12 – *...the gospel I preached is not of human origin. ...I received it by revelation from Jesus Christ.*

Paul's gospel came directly from the glorified, resurrected Christ. It wasn't filtered through anybody's opinion or skewed by anyone's interpretation. He got it straight from God Himself. It was a message of such complete and total grace that people actually thought if they lived a sinful life under grace, then God would be glorified because it would highlight His graciousness even more.

> **Romans 6:1-2** – *What shall we say, then? Shall we go on sinning so that grace may increase? By no means!*

> **Romans 6:15** – *What then? Shall we sin because we are not under the law but under grace? By no means!*

Paul says, "No way!" Grace doesn't keep us rooted in the weed-filled wasteland of sin. Under grace we get uprooted and replanted permanently in the ever-blooming garden of Jesus. Our roots now sink down into His unfailing love and we are nourished by the waters of righteousness that flow from His throne. Just because we have been removed from the prison of sin doesn't mean we will be able to live sin-free lives. We will always be a work in progress. There will always be areas we need to grow in and things we need to change. **Grace releases power for us to grow because it gives us the freedom to fail and to never be condemned when we do.** The more we really understand what grace is and what it means in our lives, the more we learn how to break our sin habits.

> **Titus 2:11-12** – *For the grace of God...teaches us to say "No" to ungodliness and worldly passions...*

Those of us who think that grace is dangerous because it allows us to get away with whatever we want do not trust that God will win us over with this amazing grace. Out of fear we feel we must threaten with condemnation those who don't conform to the rules, expectations, or standards we think the Bible puts on us.

Paul also gives us rules, expectations, and standards, but he does so in the context of grace. The Bible spells out in great detail how we should live.

> **Ephesians 4:2-3** – *Be completely humble and gentle; be patient, bearing with one another in love. Make every effort to keep the unity of the Spirit through the bond of peace.*

Philippians 2:14 – *Do everything without grumbling or arguing...*

Colossians 3:8 – *But now you must also rid yourselves of all such things as these: anger, rage, malice, slander, and filthy language from your lips.*

These are just a few samples of many and we should always do our best to follow the Bible's directions and instructions under the guidance of the Holy Spirit. We should also be eager to allow the Holy Spirit to use others to speak truth into our lives, to tell us the treasures that are in us as well as the areas we could grow in.

Paul does not dishonor the price paid for us by threatening that Jesus' blood will not cover us if we go too far in the wrong direction. Religion does that by putting limits on grace and inferring that what Jesus did for us was not complete—that there are still sins for which the penalty has been left unpaid. This is an insult to the suffering and punishment Christ endured on our behalf. It says that what He did was not good enough and that we must make up the difference with our own obedience.

Paul's grace message was "all of Jesus and none of us." At one point he brought his grace message to the leaders in Jerusalem to confirm he was on the right track.

Galatians 2:2, 6 – *...meeting privately with those esteemed as leaders, I presented to them the gospel that I preach among the Gentiles. I wanted to be sure I was not running and had not been running my race in vain. ...they added nothing to my message.*

They didn't correct or change anything he was teaching people about the grace of Christ. Instead, they encouraged him to keep going and to fulfill the mission that God had given him to win the Gentiles with God's undeserved favor.

It's Greek to Me

As we saw in previous chapters, the Greek word translated *saved* means more than being rescued from hell. It also includes "to preserve from danger,"[36] "to be healed," "to be delivered," and "to be made whole" amongst other things. In this verse, the verb is in the present tense, which means it is something that is happening continually. The Corinthians were saved when they believed the gospel Paul preached to them, so for it to mean that they were currently and continually being saved as they *"hold firmly"* to it is inconsistent with how Paul describes salvation in other verses.

> **Ephesians 2:8** – *For it is by grace you have been saved, through faith...*

The tense of the verb *saved* here is perfect. Perfect tense means that something has happened at a point in time in the past, and the result of that action continues into the present. The Corinthians, like the Ephesians, already received salvation through faith. When they did, they were delivered from condemnation. The result of that deliverance continues on indefinitely. It is inconsistent for Paul to describe salvation in the perfect tense, where it has already occurred and its results continue on into the present, and then to change it to the present tense where it depends on what we do right now.

It can't be both, so in our topic verse Paul must be referring to another aspect of salvation other than going to heaven. Given the context of the verse, "to be made whole" fits nicely.

The verb phrase translated *hold firmly* means "to keep, retain, or hold on to."[37] It is in the present active tense which means that they are to initiate the action of holding on to the message and to keep holding on to it. The King James Version translates it *"keep in memory."* The implication here is that Paul wants them to remind themselves of the gospel over and over in order to keep it fresh in their minds.

The word used for *in vain* does not mean "for nothing" but rather "without cause or purpose."[38] It does not indicate that their faith wouldn't be able to save them; rather, it implies that their faith would not accomplish the purpose that God intended. The same word is used later in the chapter to describe the purpose of God's grace in Paul's life.

> **1 Corinthians 15:10-11** – *But by the grace of God I am what I am, and his grace to me was not without effect (in vain). No, I worked harder than all of them—yet not I, but the grace of God that was with me. Whether, then, it is I or they, this is what we preach, and this is what you believed. (brackets mine)*

The grace of God compelled Paul to work hard at spreading the good news. He was so moved by God's undeserved favor in his life that he couldn't help but give everything he had to tell others about it. He wants the good news of grace to have this same effect in their lives, so he implores them to keep the message of grace fresh in their minds and on their hearts.

Found in Translation

One way this verse could be translated in order to convey the meaning Paul intended, and not to contradict what grace is, might be

> "By this gospel you are being made whole if you constantly remind yourselves of the word I preached to you. Otherwise, your belief has no purpose."

By constantly reminding ourselves of the good news of God's grace, we are filled with faith, hope, love, peace, joy, etc. Undeserved favor from the Creator of the universe has a way of making us happy. What makes us happy will usually find its way out of our mouths and into the ears of those around us. Let us remind ourselves over and over of what He has done by reading the Bible through grace lenses, listening to grace-filled messages, reading grace-based books, being in fellowship with other grace-filled believers, and living in a way that is consistent with who He made us to be.

CHAPTER 20:
HE WILL DISOWN YOU

2 Timothy 2:11-13 – *Here is a trustworthy saying: If we died with him, we will also live with him; if we endure, we will also reign with him. If we disown him, he will also disown us; if we are faithless, he will remain faithful, for he cannot disown himself.*

Scratching the Surface

This passage seems very confusing. Especially the part that says, *"If we disown him, he will also disown us; if we are faithless, he will remain faithful."* Huh?! God will disown us but at the same time He will remain faithful? These two things sound completely opposite. Also, what if we don't endure? Does that mean we won't reign with Him? What does it mean to endure? How much endurance is required for us to reign with Him?

Law vs. Grace

Here is a trustworthy saying: these verses are very perplexing! They seem to imply that two opposing truths exist at the same time, which actually isn't uncommon for God to do. He often gives us spiritual truths that contradict our earthly logic and reason. For example, we must die to live, we must give to receive, the least shall be the greatest, etc. But when it comes to grace and the law, that is "once saved, always saved" vs. "measure up or be condemned," there is no paradox. There is no mixture of these in the New Covenant. The Old Covenant already mixed law and grace and it was called the ministry of death. In the New Covenant we say, "been there, done that."

Is disowning Jesus a sin? Of course. Was Jesus already punished for that sin regardless of when it occurs? Yes, He was. Because God is holy and just, He cannot punish the same sin twice. That's why it is impossible for us to lose our salvation. All sin has already been punished.

That's not to say that there aren't consequences when we willfully sin. There absolutely are, but one of the consequences can never be condemnation. Jesus took that option off the table when He was punished in our place. This is known as the finished work of the cross. We no longer work to receive the eternal reward of salvation. We are no longer eternally judged by what we do. We are now eternally judged only by whether we accept His payment for all of our sins, making us forever righteous in God's eyes. If it's impossible for us to ever have any sin charged against us, then it's impossible for us to ever be unrighteous before God.

It's Greek to Me

Let's look more closely at the first challenging part of this passage, *"if we endure, we will also reign with him,"* where it seems to say that if we don't endure, then we won't reign with Him. The Greek word for *endure* is a combination of two words.

- Hupo: properly, *under*, often meaning *under* authority of someone; working *directly* as a subordinate (*under* someone/something else).

- Menó: to stay, abide, remain[39]

Enduring implies that we are persevering through persecution, trials, or challenges, but this passage is not speaking of these things. Paul is taking a break from his instructions to Timothy to make generic, individual statements of spiritual truths. The context of this particular statement is reigning or ruling with Jesus. We typically associate reigning with Jesus with His Second Coming, which is true, but we also reign in this life right now.

> **Romans 5:17** – *For if, by the trespass of the one man, death reigned through that one man, how much more will those who receive God's abundant provision of grace and of the gift of righteousness **reign in life** through the one man, Jesus Christ! (emphasis mine)*

We reign in life right now because of *"God's abundant provision of grace and of the gift of righteousness."* When we are under the authority of God's grace (hupo) we are kings with Jesus and we rule over this life with Him. As we stay or dwell in this place of submission to Jesus (menó) as both our Savior and Lord, we will continue to reign with Him over this life. When we rebel against Him and do not live in our true identity as kings, then we allow the things of this life and this world to rule over us.

Our next difficult statement, *"If we disown him, he will also disown us,"* appears to imply that He will cut us off from salvation if we renounce Him as our Messiah. While on the surface this seems fair, it is not consistent with grace covering all of our sins. Certainly disowning Jesus would be a sin; as such, grace means that the penalty of condemnation for this sin has already been paid on the cross. Since God, in His perfect holiness, justice, and righteousness, cannot punish the same sin twice, it is impossible for Him to charge us as guilty and sentence us to hell for it. Therefore, this statement must mean something other than what it appears to mean.

The Greek word translated "disown" is *arneomai* and means "to deny, to say no."[40] It is impossible for us to disown Jesus and for Jesus to disown us. We are permanently fused together as a new creation. We cannot get out of being in Christ, and He cannot get out of being in us. We can, however, say no to Him when He gives us instructions. The reason we say no is because we want to do our own thing, but in denying Him we will also be denied satisfaction. We will never find joy in going our own way. God loves us too much to let our hearts be fulfilled through rebellion.

Another way we can view this statement is in the same light as a similar passage.

> **Matthew 10:32-33** – *(Jesus speaking) "Whoever acknowledges me before others, I will also acknowledge before my Father in heaven. But whoever disowns me before others, I will disown before my Father in heaven."*

Here Jesus is sending out the twelve apostles to heal the sick and drive out demons. After giving them instructions for their task, He then continues to prophesy spiritual truths, including these two verses. They are very similar to the passage we are studying, the key difference being the pronoun *whoever* vs. *we*. In these verses, Jesus is referring to whoever will confess or deny Him as their Lord and Savior. If any of us acknowledge Jesus as Lord, He will acknowledge us as His before the Father. If we deny Him as Lord, then He will deny us before the Father. It goes back to the only sin that will prevent us from being saved—blaspheming the Holy Spirit—which is refusing to accept Jesus.

The same word for *disown* or *deny* is also used in an even stronger form when Jesus tells Peter that Peter will deny Him three times. When Peter did that, did Jesus disown him? Not at all. Jesus did not erase Peter's name from the Book of Life, turn His back on him, and let him walk off into oblivion. It is simply not what Jesus, or the passage in 2 Timothy, means.

In our subject text, Paul uses *we*, so we automatically assume he is referring to Christians. But he is breaking from specifically addressing Timothy here and inserting general statements of kingdom truths. He is using *we* in a generic sense, meaning mankind. He is repeating what Jesus said above. If we, meaning anyone, deny Jesus as Lord, then He will deny us salvation because we have blasphemed the Holy Spirit. When we accept His grace, then we are His forever.

Once we are in Him, we are one with Him. If He disowned or denied us, in the sense of canceling our salvation, He would be disowning or denying Himself. We are His because He purchased us. He paid a ransom for us, and we now belong to Him for eternity. **Nothing can overcome the power of the blood to hold on to what it bought.**

In the next statement, Paul says that the Lord remains faithful even when we do not. This is the essence of grace. No matter how our faith fails, even if we haven't yet accepted Jesus, He stays with us, He continues to encourage us, He will even discipline us if necessary, but He will always be faithful to the goal of getting us to be with Him for eternity as well as to live out our true identity on earth. He does so because that is His nature. If He contradicted His nature, He would be denying Himself. He has no choice but to be faithful because that is simply who He is.

Found in Translation

This passage can easily lead us to form incorrect conclusions that we can lose our salvation if we don't endure or if we deny Jesus in some way, but with just a little effort and with the help of the Holy Spirit, we can re-work it to be consistent with grace. One possible way of translating the verses could be

> **2 Timothy 2:11-13** – *Here is a trustworthy saying: If we died with Him, we will also live with Him; if we stay under [His rule], we will also rule with Him. If we say no to Him [as Lord], He will also say no to us [as being our Lord]; if we are faithless, He will remain faithful, for He cannot deny Himself.*

In this way, it is a little easier to keep New Covenant grace in tact while staying true to what was written.

CHAPTER 21:
REPENTANCE IMPOSSIBLE

Hebrews 6:4-6 – *It is impossible for those who have once been enlightened, who have tasted the heavenly gift, who have shared in the Holy Spirit, who have tasted the goodness of the word of God and the powers of the coming age, if they fall away, to be brought back to repentance, because to their loss they are crucifying the Son of God all over again and subjecting him to public disgrace.*

Scratching the Surface

This is a very scary passage that appears to indicate if we turn away from God it is impossible to repent. It sounds like repentance that brings salvation is a one-shot deal, and if we mess up and get off track somewhere down the road, we lose our salvation. Plus, we couldn't get it back if we wanted to because we would have to crucify *"the Son of God all over again."*

But how far off track is too far? What does it mean to *fall away*? Is it when we stop going to church, stop praying for a certain amount of time, or verbally renounce Jesus as our Lord?

Law vs. Grace

When Jesus was arrested to be crucified, Peter did not just renounce Jesus as his Lord. He went one step beyond that. He verbally renounced even knowing Jesus—not once, but three times. The second time he did it, Peter made an oath in front of the crowd, promising them that he didn't know Him. The third time, Peter took it another step further.

> **Matthew 26:74** – *Then he began to call down curses, and he swore to them, "I don't know the man!"*

He could not get more emphatic about denying Jesus than by swearing it to them as well as cursing himself if he was lying, which he obviously was. In Peter's state of panic, he completely and vehemently disowned Jesus. He couldn't say it or do it more strongly or forcefully if he tried.

After Jesus died and rose again, the New Covenant of grace took over. One of the first things Jesus did was restore Peter's faith and demonstrate the all-consuming power of grace over every sin. He shows us right out of the tomb that no matter how faithless we become and no matter what mistakes we make, He remains faithful and our sins (past, present, and future) have been totally removed from us. Nothing is held against us, not even swearing and cursing that we don't know Him at all.

If Peter, someone who actually walked with Jesus as a friend and a disciple for three years, could renounce Jesus in such a demonstrative manner and yet still be totally forgiven, even restored to the point of leading the entire church, how could we be held to a higher standard when we only know Him by faith? How could we ever be condemned for falling away when Peter wasn't?

Religion tells us that we will be condemned for *apostasy*, which is a fancy word meaning "to renounce one's faith" or "to abandon a previous loyalty."[41] Peter committed apostasy, but instead of sentencing Peter to hell, Jesus brought him to repentance (i.e. changed his mind), and then reinstated him as an apostle. As a result of his restoration, Peter ended up preaching the very first sermon in the age of the New Covenant, he performed many miracles including having his shadow heal the sick, he was the source of Mark's gospel, and he wrote the books of First and Second Peter.

Some of us might think that if Peter had not repented, he would have eventually lost his salvation. This reasoning discounts and discredits the cross. Either Jesus measured up to perfection and was an acceptable sacrifice on our behalf, or He wasn't. If He was, we are free. If He wasn't, we stand condemned because it is impossible for us to make up for anything Jesus lacked.

We can no longer allow the enemy to use the Bible against us via religion. **The threat of losing our salvation for any reason is nothing but Satan trying to put us under the law and prevent us from living in our true identity and in our full inheritance.**

It's Greek to Me

The writer of Hebrews transitions from speaking directly to his audience in verses 1-3 with the use of first person plural pronouns like *us* and *we* to using third person plural pronouns like *those* and *they* in verses 4-6. He stops talking to and about the Hebrew believers for a moment and starts speaking about people who are not in the fellowship anymore—people who have wandered away from the truth.

Some of us might think that the reason the writer switched to third person pronouns is because the people he is talking about are no longer Christians. They left the church and thus left God, leaving their salvation behind. And yes, on the surface it appears that way. That thinking cannot be reconciled with Peter being restored, with Jesus having paid for all sin, and with the definition of grace being undeserved favor. It goes against the entire premise of the New Covenant.

In most translations, this passage begins with the word *for* which means that the writer is "expressing the reason, cause, motive, principle, etc. of what has been previously said."[42] For some reason, the NIV left this out which is unfortunate because it makes an important connection between what was just said and what is about to be said. In the prior verses, the author of Hebrews makes some important points to build upon.

> **Hebrews 6:1-3** – *Therefore let us move beyond the elementary teachings about Christ and be taken forward to maturity, not laying again the foundation of repentance from acts that lead to death [or from dead works], and of faith in God, instruction about cleansing rites [or about baptisms], the laying on of hands, the resurrection of the dead, and eternal judgment. And God permitting, we will do so. (brackets mine)*

In verses 1-3, the writer is talking about us moving on from *"elementary teachings"* and *"not laying again the foundation of repentance from acts that lead to death."* Literally, *"acts that lead to death"* should be translated *dead works* as it is in other versions. It refers to us being under the law and attempting to obtain our own righteousness through works and obedience. They are dead works because they will never produce the eternal life we are striving for. They are fruitless deeds, not because we or others don't benefit from them, but because they can't ever make us good enough to stand blameless before the throne. The writer is establishing that salvation by grace is a basic teaching of the church, and that we are done with a works-based system. After all, he's writing to Hebrews (Jews) who were just coming out from under the law and were totally works oriented.

"For it is impossible" would be the same as us saying "Because it is impossible." He is stating the reason why he thinks they should move on from the basic teachings. Specifically, he is referring to someone being *"brought back to repentance"* after having experienced salvation and then falling away from grace to being back under the law. **In essence, he is saying, "Let's move on from teaching about repentance from dead works because it is impossible for someone to do it over."**

Repenting from dead works means changing our minds from believing we have to measure up to a standard in order to be good enough for salvation to believing in what Jesus did for us. Once we change our minds and come to accept Jesus as our Savior, we enter into the New Covenant of grace. No sin will ever be counted against us again, even if we renounce our faith and fall away like Peter did.

> **Galatians 5:4** – *You who are trying to be justified by the law have been alienated from Christ; you have fallen away from grace.*

Falling away does not mean we lose our salvation. When we fall away from grace, we put ourselves back under the law, but it does not cancel the covenant we are already a party to. It simply means we are not living in our true identity and in our full inheritance. It means we started believing the enemy's lie again that God isn't really as good as the gospel of grace makes Him seem. It's the same lie he used in the garden. The truth is that He is that good because He paid the highest price possible to be able to be with us forever. He created an eternal covenant that can never be broken. The grace covenant we are under is eternal because the blood that established it is eternal.

It is impossible to bring us back to this repentance because it was this change of mind that took us from trusting in ourselves to trusting in Jesus, thus entering us into the New Covenant...one time for all time. We can't do it over. We can't be *"brought back"* to it. We already did it. It's a done deal.

When Jesus restored Peter, Peter did not have to be re-saved. His faith just needed to be renewed. If we had to be re-saved every time we fell away, we could never be sure of our salvation. Never does the Bible talk about someone needing to be re-converted because they fell away. When we are converted, it is once and for all because Jesus died once and for all. If being saved one time wasn't enough to save us forever, then Jesus did not take away all of our sin on the cross, and He would have to be crucified again and again until it's all paid for. He would also need to be put to public shame again.

The point of this passage all boils down to this: We are saved one time for all time, so it's impossible for us to do it again. Jesus was crucified one time for all time, so it's impossible for Him to do it again.

Now this brings us to the troubling couple of verses which follow.

> **Hebrews 6:7-8** – *Land that drinks in the rain often falling on it and that produces a crop useful to those for whom it is farmed receives the blessing of God. But land that produces thorns and thistles is worthless and is in danger of being cursed. In the end it will be burned.*

Now this sounds like if we receive God's love and mercy and are fruitful in a way that's useful to Him then we will be blessed, but if we aren't then in the end we will go to hell. If we misinterpreted the previous verses to mean that once we fall away it's impossible to repent, so we will be lost, this little parable would appear to confirm that fallacy.

It is true that as we continually receive God's love and mercy, as illustrated by *"the rain often falling on it,"* and produce a useful crop that God will pour out more blessings in our lives. We are proving ourselves to be good stewards of what He is investing into us, and as a result He can trust us with even more. This is a common theme throughout the Bible.

The opposite is true as well. If He is raining down His goodness on us and we are producing nothing but *"thorns and thistles,"* which is a picture of the results of sin, then we will be *"in danger of being cursed."* We see an example of this in the parable of The Lost Son (Luke 15:11-32). He took his inheritance (rain) and wasted it in self indulgence (thorns and thistles). A famine came (cursed) and he found himself so hungry he wanted to eat pig slop (burned). The result wasn't being condemned to burn in hell. No, his father was eager to welcome him back.

It is common for farmers to burn a field of thorns and thistles in order to clean it, purify it, and fertilize it with the ash so that it will become a fruitful field. In this case, God is the farmer and we are the field.

> **Isaiah 10:17** – *The Lord, the Light of Israel, will be a fire; the Holy One will be a flame. He will devour the thorns and briers with fire, burning up the enemy in a single night. (NLT)*

We can rebel to the point where it is necessary for God to burn our thorn bushes. Being burned is painful. The Lost Son was starving to death before he was sufficiently burned. If that's what it takes for us to say, "Enough is enough! I'm going back home," then our loving Farmer Daddy is willing to discipline us for our own good.

> **Hebrews 12:11** – *No discipline seems pleasant at the time, but painful. Later on, however, it produces a harvest of righteousness and peace for those who have been trained by it.*

Discipline is designed to bring us to the end of our false identity by revealing who we really are and whose we really are in Christ. If we are indulging in the things of the world after we have received Jesus, we don't know who we really are. We are believing a lie about our identity as well as a lie about how perfectly loved we are right now. The *"harvest of righteousness and peace"* comes from receiving a revelation that we are completely righteous through our faith in Jesus. As a result, an eternal peace settles in our hearts. The degree to which we embrace this revelation is the degree to which we accept ourselves for who He made us to be, empowering us to use the rain and produce a crop useful to the Kingdom.

> **Isaiah 55:13** – *Where once there were thorns, cypress trees will grow. Where nettles grew, myrtles will sprout up. These events will bring great honor to the Lord's name; they will be an everlasting sign of his power and love. (NLT)*

It is to the Lord's glory that He rids us of thorns and thistles in order to establish strong trees that are useful to Him. He gets the praise when He turns our failure into success, when He transforms us from victim to victor. It would only bring disgrace to His name if He was not able to save us out of our mess after we called upon Him at one point. That is simply not the nature *"of His power and love"* which supply the grace that we do not deserve.

Found in Translation

The challenges with this passage do not lie with it being mistranslated; rather, with it being misinterpreted because we are not looking at it through the lenses of grace. If we do not have a solid grasp on the elementary teachings, including salvation being a one-time event that happens with repentance from dead works where we enter into the New Covenant of grace once and for all, then it is easy to develop incorrect theology that puts us under the law. The surface meaning contradicts both Peter's falling away as well as the parable of The Lost Son, not to mention the very definition of grace.

By seeing the Scriptures through grace lenses, we can make sense of difficult passages like this and maintain our confidence in the finished work of the cross.

CHAPTER 22:
FAITH AND DEEDS

James 2:14-26 – *What good is it, my brothers, if a man claims to have faith but has no deeds? Can such faith save him?*

Suppose a brother or sister is without clothes and daily food. If one of you says to him, "Go, I wish you well; keep warm and well fed," but does nothing about his physical needs, what good is it? In the same way, faith by itself, if it is not accompanied by action, is dead.

But someone will say, "You have faith; I have deeds." Show me your faith without deeds, and I will show you my faith by what I do. You believe that there is one God. Good! Even the demons believe that—and shudder.

You foolish man, do you want evidence that faith without deeds is useless? Was not our ancestor Abraham considered righteous for what he did when he offered his son Isaac on the altar? You see that his faith and his actions were working together, and his faith was made complete by what he did. And the scripture was fulfilled that says, "Abraham believed God, and it was credited to him as righteousness," and he was called God's friend. You see that a person is justified by what he does and not by faith alone.

In the same way, was not even Rahab the prostitute considered righteous for what she did when she gave lodging to the spies and sent them off in a different direction? As the body without the spirit is dead, so faith without deeds is dead.

Scratching the Surface

This sure doesn't sound the gospel of grace. Aren't we saved by faith and not by works? Yet this passage seems to imply that if our faith does not produce deeds, we do not have enough faith to be saved. If this were true then we must ask how many good works are enough? Where is the cut off point? Is God keeping score? If we don't hit the minimum number of good deeds then will we be condemned? How can this passage be true and at the same time Paul's statement in Ephesians be true?

> **Ephesians 4:8-9** – *For it is by grace you have been saved, through faith — and this not from yourselves, it is the gift of God — not by works, so that no one can boast.*

These verses (as well as others) seem to contradict what James is saying. So how do we reconcile these opposing messages?

Law vs. Grace

Some of us can have almost a rebellious attitude toward the expectation that we should do good works since we are saved by grace. We don't like anyone putting that kind of responsibility on us. It can make us feel like we are not good enough the way we are and that we have to earn our acceptance by meeting some standard. That's a good thing in some ways. We are sensitive to religion trying to make our salvation about what we do instead of it being about a secure, intimate relationship with our unconditionally loving Father. Perhaps we came out of a religious environment where we felt abused and rejected, where we never measured up, and now we bristle at the thought of having any kind of expectation to put our faith into action.

On the flip side, some of us read a passage like this one in James and feel that if people say they are Christians but their faith is not producing good deeds we question if they are really saved. We like passages like this because they set an expectation for how we are to live and how we are to make a difference in this world. If someone isn't living up to these "biblical standards," we can easily conclude that their faith isn't real. It gives us a measuring stick to judge whether people are truly following Jesus or just want salvation without needing to repent.

Both of these positions are a distortion of the truth. James is writing to the first group, and Paul is writing to the second. James is writing to those who can use grace as an excuse to be lazy and selfish, and Paul is writing to those who still have law-based, judgmental thinking toward anyone who is not doing enough. The idea in James 2 that we are not justified by faith alone but, rather, by faith and works (or deeds) is just as true as Paul's statement that we are justified by faith alone.

No matter what side of the camp we are on, one thing is clear. How we walk out our faith is very important.

> **Ephesians 2:10** – *For we are God's handiwork, created in Christ Jesus to do good works, which God prepared in advance for us to do.*

> **Matthew 5:16** – *(Jesus speaking) "...let your light shine before men, that they may see your good deeds and praise your Father in heaven."*

There are many verses that talk about putting our faith into practice and performing good works, but **we must understand from God's perspective how faith and deeds work together in a way that doesn't undermine grace.** Grace says that we are perfectly loved and accepted just the way we are, and that nothing is required of us to be saved. The law says that we must do something to prove that our faith is real, otherwise our salvation is in question.

The more we understand grace, the more we can't help but want to share the love and mercy we receive from Him. Each of us is at a different place in our journey and on our own unique path. Some of us have come from very painful and challenging pasts and we will need a lot more time to heal before we can really start pouring ourselves out to others who are hurting. Others of us have come from relatively healthy pasts and it is no problem for us to jump into serving and ministering. "Just because it's different, doesn't mean it's wrong." God meets us where we are and walks with us in a positive direction.

If we are not basking in the warm, gooey, goodness of God's unconditional love and approval to the point where we overflow with it, then the good deeds we do are most likely motivated out of our own desire to feel accepted by God. It is a downward spiral of constantly seeking approval, creating more insecurity in our relationship with Him and more critical attitudes towards others who are not trying as hard as we are.

The important thing is to ask Daddy what we can do given where we are in our walk. If we have received the gifts of salvation and righteousness, we have received something we can share in a healthy way if it is motivated by love. It could be something as small as saying, "Good morning," to the cashier at the coffee shop or it could be praying for someone to be healed in the grocery store. It doesn't matter as long as it is coming from a place of freely giving what we have freely received.

Galatians 5:6 – *...The only thing that counts is faith expressing itself through love.*

This expression of faith constitutes good deeds. **Works and deeds are not for us to become righteous or justified in God's eyes, but to show the world what people are like who are in a right relationship with God.** They are also meant to move us further down the path of being more like Jesus.

The faith that James is talking about naturally and effortlessly produces good works. It comes from living in a place where we are in tune with the Spirit and flowing with the desires of our Father. Our hearts are set on His will, and we are looking for ways to do good, bubbling over with love from Him. We are open to Him leading us to opportunities *"which God prepared in advance for us to do."*

It's Greek to Me

When James asks, "Can such faith save him?" we must stop and remind ourselves of where our faith comes from in the first place. As we discussed in an earlier chapter, our faith in Jesus is a gift from God. If faith for salvation comes from God and James is questioning if we have enough faith for salvation because we don't have works, then James would be accusing our Father of not supplying us with enough faith to be saved. James is more in tune with God than that. He must be trying to say something else.

In the phrase, "Can such faith save him?" the word for "can" is *dunamai* and it means "divine power or ability."[43] Unfortunately, most translators seem satisfied with just using the word "can."

Also, as we have seen before, the word for *save* means other things than just being delivered from condemnation. In the context of this passage where James is challenging believers to put their faith into action to show that it's alive, it will cause them to be made more whole as a result. **James is speaking more to our lack of power to prosper spiritually when we are without deeds than he is to our insufficient faith for salvation.**

In verses 17 and 25 where James says, *"faith without deeds is dead,"* it does not mean that our faith is false or that it doesn't exist. If it did, that would imply that we were not in right standing with our Father in heaven which is not what James is trying to say. The word *dead* in this instance means that without deeds our faith is "destitute of force or power, inactive, inoperative."[44] Verse 20 confirms this saying, *"faith without deeds is useless,"* where the word *useless* literally means "inactive, idle, lazy."[45] **He is saying that without deeds, our faith becomes useless in our own lives and in the lives of those around us.** He is imploring us to revive our faith with deeds because it can be a very effective means of getting us moving in the right direction when we have become idle and lazy in God's abundant grace.

In verse 24 where James says, *"You see that a person is justified by what he does and not by faith alone,"* he is not referring to works being necessary to be saved. The word *justified* is in the present tense which means that it has already happened and it continues to happen. It is progressive. We know from other verses that we are justified for salvation by accepting the gift Jesus' blood purchased, apart from works. We just receive it by faith (faith that we received from God). So James isn't complicating the process of becoming a Christian with this verse, nor is he contradicting what Jesus or Paul have said elsewhere. **He is saying that as we do good works we will continue to experience greater measures of justification than if we just believe and do nothing.** More and more justification is added to the justification we have already received when we first believed. Helps Word Study puts it this way

> The believer is "made righteous/justified" (*dikaióō*) by the Lord, cleared of all charges (punishment) related to their sins. Moreover, they are justified (*dikaióō*) "made right," "righteous" by God's grace each time they receive (obey) faith.[46]

When we get our couch potato faith off the sofa and into action, it's spiritual exercise; our faith gets stronger, we have more spiritual endurance, we overcome temptations easier, we have more fruits of the Spirit, etc. That's why James is challenging Christians to put their faith into practice. He wants us overflowing with the security of God's love and power, walking boldly into difficult situations and watching heaven show up to bring peace where there was anxiety a minute ago, to bring healing to the sick, to bring hope to the hopeless, etc. When we don't overflow with Him, the opposite happens, and no one benefits except the enemy. We feel more tempted, weak, and insecure. We are not confident that we can make any kind of difference. We will either spiral up or spiral down but whether we take action or not does not depend on us alone. **It depends on Him in us**.

Bill Johnson says, "You are to be a river and not a lake. He is to flow through you."[47]

Pastor Joseph Prince says, "Right believing leads to right living."[48]

The more we choose to worship, praise, and meditate on how much we are loved and celebrated by Him, the more His faith and His presence will be with us, on us, in us, and working through us.

Found in Translation

Some of the verses that seem more contradictory to grace could be translated in a way that could easily make them less so.

> Verse 14 – What is gained, my brothers, if anyone says they have faith but they don't have works? Is this faith able to make him whole?

> Verse 17 – So also, if faith does not have works, it does nothing [to help anyone].

> Verse 24 – You see that a man is justified even more with works than just with faith alone.

> Verse 26 – Indeed, just as the body apart from the spirit is lifeless, so faith apart from works is lifeless.

Now we have less confusion with regard to works being necessary to prove that our faith is alive enough to save us. Since God gives us the faith to be saved, we do not have to prove it. He will continue to work in us so that we will become more and more of who He made us to be.

> **Philippians 1:6** – *being confident...that he who began a good work in you will carry it on to completion until the day of Christ Jesus.*

God began the work of transforming our lives from wandering orphans to beloved children, and He will continue to mature us to be more like Christ as we allow Him to lead us into every good work He has planned for us. As Paul says, let us be confident of this.

Chapter 23:
The Final Word

If Jesus paid the price for all sin, for all people, for all time, then once we enter into the New Covenant of grace there is nothing that can ever separate us from Him. We can't out sin His grace. We can't give back, throw away, or use up His gift of righteousness. We can't undo our adoption into the Royal Family.

What we can do is fully and completely enjoy the freedom and security of His unfailing love to draw closer and closer to Him. We can walk in the power and authority He has given us, destroying the works of the devil and releasing the kingdom of God into people's lives. We can accept people for who they are and for where they are in their journey without feeling the need to judge them. We can love others like He loves us, freely giving the grace that we have freely received.

If we run across passages in the New Testament that seem to contradict grace, and appear to imply that we can lose our salvation, then we must know that they are being mistranslated, misinterpreted, or misunderstood. It is a deception of the enemy to attempt to put us back under the law so that we will take our eyes off of what Jesus did for us and put them back on our own performance, empowering sin to rule over us. It is better for us to have unanswered questions about confusing Bible passages than to have the wrong answers. That is how false doctrines get formed. The Holy Spirit will reveal the right answers at the right time.

The New Covenant is an eternal covenant, established with the eternal blood of Jesus. When we enter into it we are forever cleansed, placed permanently in Christ, and look just like Jesus to our heavenly Father. Our identity is Jesus. We are in Him, and He is in us. We are one. Even while we remain on earth, we are like Him.

1 John 4:17 *...as He is, so also are we in this world. (NASB)*

Is He forever righteous? So are we in this world. Is He over all things? So are we in this world. Is He eternally healthy? So are we in this world. Is He rich beyond measure? So are we in this world. Anything that describes Jesus in heaven describes us in this world. Whatever Jesus is and whatever Jesus has is ours not when we get to heaven, but now…in this world.

I bless you with the faith and the change of mind to believe and walk in this powerful reality of grace, living and loving like Jesus—our God, our Savior, our Brother.

Amen and amen!

GROUP DISCUSSION GUIDE

Introduction

1. Share one thing that really stuck out to you from this chapter.

2. Have you ever felt condemned, judged or oppressed by religion?

    a. If so, when and how?

    b. Does it still affect your perspective of God?

3. How can we take a stand for what's right but not judge or condemn people when we do?

4. What passages in the Bible can make you insecure about your salvation?

Chapter 1 – Context of the Old Covenant

   1.   Talk about something you learned from this reading.

   2.   How has your perspective of the Old Covenant changed?

   3.   Have you ever been in a relationship that was performance based?

       a.   How did it make you feel?

       b.   How would you describe the emotional intimacy?

   4.   Did you ever mess something up by trying to make it better?

   5.   Have you ever tried to run away from God?

       a.   How did He chase you down and win you over?

Chapter 2 – Context of the Gospels

1. What's your biggest "take away" from this chapter?

2. How has your perspective of the Gospels changed?

3. Have you ever tried to live up to certain standards in an attempt to be accepted by God?

   a. How do you still do that?

4. What miraculous signs have you seen or experienced by God's grace?

5. Do you feel comfortable coming to Jesus just as you are or do you sometimes feel you need to get your act together first? Why or why not?

Chapter 3 – Context of the New Covenant

1. Discuss any "ah-ha" moments you had from this chapter.

2. How has your perspective of the New Covenant changed?

3. Talk about a time when you felt like you had lost your salvation?

4. Have you ever felt there were particular sins that disqualified people from being Christians?

   a. How does that fit with grace?

5. Do you ever feel that God is mad at you because you just aren't measuring up to His expectations?

6. What do you think about being chosen before time even began?

Chapter 4 – Once and For All

1. Talk about a point from this chapter that changed your thinking.

2. Share your thoughts on God choosing to forget all of your sins.

3. Do you tend to focus more on your shortcomings or on what Jesus has done for you?

4. How did your perspective of sin change when you found out the word "sin" is a noun and not a verb?

5. Describe your feelings about being permanently in Christ and Him being permanently in you.

6. Share how the phrase, "once a child of God, always a child of God" could alter or has altered your relationship with the Father.

Chapter 5 – The Unforgiveable Sin

1. Discuss what impacted you most about this chapter.

2. Can you think of a sin someone could commit against you that you wouldn't be able to forgive?

    a. Has it already happened?

    b. Is there anyone you still struggle to forgive? For what?

3. What are your thoughts about the cross forgiving all the sins of the whole world and not just Christians?

    a. Write out what you could say to a pre-believer about the message of grace?

4. Why is it necessary for someone to accept Christ in order to be saved?

5. Have you ever thought that you blasphemed the Holy Spirit?

    a. Describe your thoughts regarding the fact that, as a Christian, you could never commit "the unforgiveable sin."

Chapter 6 – I Had Nothing to Do With It

1. Share any revelations you got when reading this chapter.

2. Talk about the idea that it was Adam's sin that condemned you in the first place.

    a. How does this change your perspective on those who are lost?

3. Before reading this chapter did you consider yourself to be righteous?

    a. Do you now? Why or why not?

    b. How is this law-based or grace-based thinking?

4. Discuss the following statement: "Even the faith we need to receive God's gifts of grace and righteousness is itself an irrevocable, perfect gift from Him."

    a. What can you do to increase your faith?

5. Share how your thoughts about repentance have changed since reading this chapter.

6. What is God trying to change your mind about?

Chapter 7 – Breaking the Law

1. What impacted you the most when you read this chapter?

2. How do you see the law at work in your life?

   a. What happens when you fail?

3. In what ways do you wish you were different?

   a. How does this thinking empower the enemy?

4. Take out a pen and a piece of paper. Each person silently pray the following: "Daddy, what do you think of me?"

   a. Be quiet for about five minutes and write what you hear the Spirit saying in your mind. Do not qualify it. Just write whatever you hear and let it flow.

   b. If you feel comfortable, share what you heard and how it makes you feel.

5. Discuss your thoughts on the following quote from this chapter: "Grace tells us we have immeasurable value and infinite worth. Our value and our worth are determined by the price paid for us. And to our Daddy, we are worth more than the precious blood of Jesus."

6. What is your response to the statement, "If sin has been condemned, there is nothing that can condemn us?"

Chapter 8 – Free But Not Lawless

1. What do you feel was highlighted to you when you read this chapter?

2. As a result of experiencing many different cultures, my wife concluded that just because something is different doesn't mean it's wrong. Describe a time at church when you encountered something different but thought it was wrong.

    a. What do you think now?

3. What are your thoughts on Paul's statement that everything is permissible?

4. Which of the following better describes the way you think…

    a. I am free to be who God made me to be because I am perfect in Christ.

    b. I really need to get my act together spiritually so God will be able to use me.

5. Freedom is based in love and love only exists when we can choose to accept or reject it. Discuss why these concepts are important in our relationship with God.

6. Under the New Covenant, how should we apply the law to our lives?

7. Compare the results of following our sinful nature with following the Spirit.

Chapter 9 – Rags to Riches

1. Talk about how this chapter impacted you.

2. Discuss Pastor Brent Lokker's statement, "To the degree you believe who you already are in Christ, you will walk in what you already have."

3. Which identity in Christ do you find the most difficult to grasp? Why? (Son/Daughter, Heir/Heiress, King/Queen, Priest/Priestess)

    a. What are you actively doing to transform your self-image into who God says you are?

4. How has your view of financial wealth changed since reading this chapter?

5. How do you or how will you offer sacrifices of praise?

Chapter 10 – Walk this Way

1. What stood out to you most in this chapter?

2. Discuss your thoughts on doing the same works Jesus did.

3. Have you or anyone you know ever been healed by God or experienced a miracle?

4. Compare the belief that miracles died out with the formation of the Bible with the belief that Christians can perform miracles through the gifts of the Spirit, like Jesus did.

5. If you are interested following Jesus in a life of supernatural ministry, what will you do or what are you doing to pursue it?

Chapter 11 – Endure to the End

1. Share something you highlighted in this chapter.

2. Have you ever or do you currently have a "line in the sand" that says if someone does this or that then they couldn't possibly be a Christian?

3. Do we go back and forth between being saved and lost depending on how we live?

4. Have you ever suffered persecution?

   a. How did Jesus rescue you from it or protect you through it?

5. How has your perspective of this Scripture changed?

   a. How has that impacted your relationship with God?

Chapter 12 – The Rocky Soil

1. What did you enjoy about this chapter?

2. Have you ever known someone who "fell away" from God?

    a. What happened to them?

3. Share a time when someone tried to discredit your faith with trick questions about God or the Bible?

4. How can you be more prepared to answer anyone who has questions?

5. How has your perspective of this Scripture changed?

    a. How has that impacted your relationship with God?

Chapter 13 – Hold to My Teaching

1. Share something you liked from this chapter.

2. What kind of accusations does the enemy try to use against you?

3. Discuss the statement, "If there was any possibility of us losing our salvation, then Jesus did not pay for every sin on the cross."

4. How do you find rest in Jesus?

5. How has your perspective of this Scripture changed?

    a. How has that impacted your relationship with God?

Chapter 14 – The True Vine

1. What did you enjoy about this chapter?

2. Are you more tempted to indulge in sin or to judge others? (This will require courage and vulnerability)

   a. What do you think is at the root of that temptation?

3. Explore the statement, "Sin loses most of its appeal when we are embraced by unconditional love."

4. How has your perspective of this Scripture changed?

   a. How has that impacted your relationship with God?

Chapter 15 – Forgiving Others

1. Share something you took away from this chapter.

2. If you find it hard to be gracious to others, it's usually a sign that you have a hard time receiving grace from God. Talk about this concept.

3. Talk about the challenges of forgiving others the way the Lord has forgiven you.

4. How has your perspective of this Scripture changed?

   a. How has that impacted your relationship with God?

Chapter 16 – Cannot Be My Disciple

1. Share something you learned from this chapter.

2. What have you given up in order be a disciple of Jesus?

3. What distracts you from being more of a disciple of Jesus?

4. What's one thing you can do in the next few days to help you grow in your power to follow Jesus?

5. How has your perspective of this Scripture changed?

   a. How has that impacted your relationship with God?

Chapter 17 – Life and Doctrine

1. Discuss what you liked about this chapter.

2. Regarding the question from the book, "Is it possible to be too undeserving to receive undeserved favor?" discuss what types of people, in your mind, are too undeserving for God's grace. (i.e. rapists, murders, homosexuals, adulterers, etc.)

3. What person or people group do you struggle to love, accept, and honor just the way they are?

4. How has your perspective of this Scripture changed?

   a. How has that impacted your relationship with God?

Chapter 18 – Same Judgment as the Devil

1. What is something that impacted you from this chapter?

2. Share a time when you were being prideful and God opposed you.

3. How do you typically respond if someone challenges or corrects you?

4. How has your perspective of this Scripture changed?

    a. How has that impacted your relationship with God?

Chapter 19 – Believed In Vain

1. Share one thing that really stuck out to you from this chapter.

2. What worldly passions has grace taught you to say no to?

3. How will you keep the message of grace fresh in your mind?

4. How has your perspective of this Scripture changed?

    a. How has that impacted your relationship with God?

Chapter 20 – He Will Disown You

1. What is something you took away from this chapter?

2. What does the "finished work of the cross" mean to you?

3. Explain how you "reign in life" right now.

4. Discuss the implications of the statement, "Because God is perfectly just, He cannot punish the same sin twice."

5. How has your perspective of this Scripture changed?

   a. How has that impacted your relationship with God?

Chapter 21 – Repentance Impossible

1. Share your thoughts on this chapter.

2. Could we ever be condemned for falling away when Peter wasn't? Why?

3. What does it really mean to "fall away"?

4. How has your perspective of this Scripture changed?

    a. How has that impacted your relationship with God?

Chapter 22 – Faith and Deeds

1. Discuss your reaction to this chapter.

2. Do you ever question someone's salvation because of their lack of works?

3. Share how doing good works impacts your faith.

4. How has your perspective of this Scripture changed?

   a. How has that impacted your relationship with God?

Chapter 23 – The Final Word

1. How did this chapter impact you?

Endnotes

1 Bono Quotes, http://christian-quotes.ochristian.com/Bono-Quotes/ (2013).

2 Johnson, Bill. Sermon, Great Grace Conference, Jubilee Christian Center, San Jose, CA, 2008.

3 Lampe, Dr. Craig H. *The Pre-Reformation History of the Bible From 1,400 BC to 1,400 AD*, http://www.greatsite.com/timeline-english-bible-history/pre-reformation.html (2013).

4 Crowder, John. Miracle Workers, Reformers, and The New Mystics (Shippensburg, PA: Destiny Image, 2006) 370.

5 Addison, Doug. Sermon, Blazing Fire Church, Livermore, CA 2010.

6 StudyLight.org, Interlinear Study Bible, http://classic.studylight.org/isb/ and GreatTreasures.org http://greattreasures.org/gnt/main.do (2013).

7 Ibid.

8 Ibid.

9 Ibid.

10 John 19:30.

11 StudyLight.org, Interlinear Study Bible, http://classic.studylight.org/isb/ and GreatTreasures.org http://greattreasures.org/gnt/main.do (2013).

12 Ibid.

13 Prince, Joseph. Sermon, Destined to Reign broadcast on ABC Family, 2011.

14 Galatians 5:16.

15 StudyLight.org, Interlinear Study Bible, http://classic.studylight.org/isb/ and GreatTreasures.org http://greattreasures.org/gnt/main.do (2013).

16 Philippians 4:7.

17 1 Peter 1:8.

18 Lokker, Brent. *Always Loved: You Are God's Treasure, Not His Project Father* (Brent Lokker Ministries, 2012), 175.

19 StudyLight.org, Interlinear Study Bible, http://classic.studylight.org/isb/ and GreatTreasures.org http://greattreasures.org/gnt/main.do (2013).

20 Ibid.

21 Ibid.

22 Johnson, Bill. Sermon, Bethel Church, Redding, CA 2013.

23 Eddie L. Hyatt. *2000 Years of Charismatic Christianity – A 21st Century Look at Church History from a Pentecostal/Charismatic Perspective* (Lake Mary FL: Charisma House 2002) 16-17.

24 Hyatt, *2000 Years of Charismatic Christianity,* 41-42.

25 Ibid., 46.

26 Ibid., 75.

27 Baker, Rolland and Heidi. Always Enough: God's Miraculous Provision among the Poorest Children on Earth. Grand Rapids, MI: Chosen Books, 2003.

28 StudyLight.org, Interlinear Study Bible, http://classic.studylight.org/isb/ and GreatTreasures.org http://greattreasures.org/gnt/main.do (2013).

ENDNOTES

[29] Ibid.

[30] Ibid.

[31] Ibid.

[32] Ibid.

[33] Ibid.

[34] Ibid.

[35] Hebrews 12:2.

[36] StudyLight.org, Interlinear Study Bible, http://classic.studylight.org/isb/ and GreatTreasures.org http://greattreasures.org/gnt/main.do (2013).

[37] Ibid.

[38] Ibid.

[39] Ibid.

[40] Ibid.

[41] Ibid.

[42] Ibid.

[43] Ibid.

[44] Ibid.

[45] Ibid.

[46] BibleHub, http://biblehub.com/ (2013).

[47] Johnson, Bill. Sermon, Great Grace Conference, Jubilee Christian Center, San Jose, CA, 2008.

[48] Prince, Joseph. Sermon, Destined to Reign broadcast on ABC Family, 2011.

Made in the USA
San Bernardino, CA
15 October 2017